COUPLES THERAPY ACTIVITY BOOK

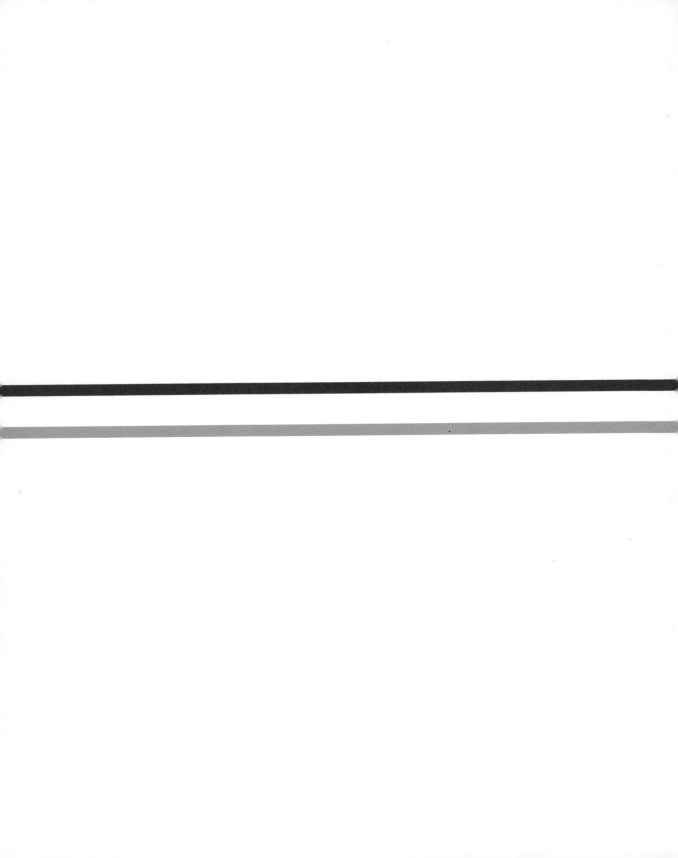

COUPLES THERAPY
ACTIVITY BOOK

65 Creative Activities to Improve Communication
and Strengthen Your Relationship

MELISSA FULGIERI, LCSW

ROCKRIDGE
PRESS

First Rockridge Press trade paperback edition 2022

Rockridge Press and the Rockridge Press logo are trademarks or registered trademarks of Callisto Media Inc. and/or its affiliates in the United States and other countries and may not be used without written permission.

For general information on our other products and services, please contact our Customer Care Department within the United States at (866) 744-2665, or outside the United States at (510) 253-0500.

Paperback ISBN: 978-1-68539-172-0 | eBook ISBN: 978-1-68539-944-3

Manufactured in the United States of America

Interior and Cover Designer: Scott A. Wooledge
Art Producer: Janice Ackerman
Editor: Andrea Leptinsky
Production Editor: Ellina Litmanovich
Production Manager: David Zapanta

Illustration courtesy of Noun Project.
Author photo courtesy of Kevin Sweeney.

10 9 8 7 6 5 4 3 2 1 0

**TO MY
HUSBAND, KEVIN.**
For your unwavering
belief in my capabilities.
For both pushing
me to endlessly grow
and accepting me as
I am. You taught me how
to love and be loved.

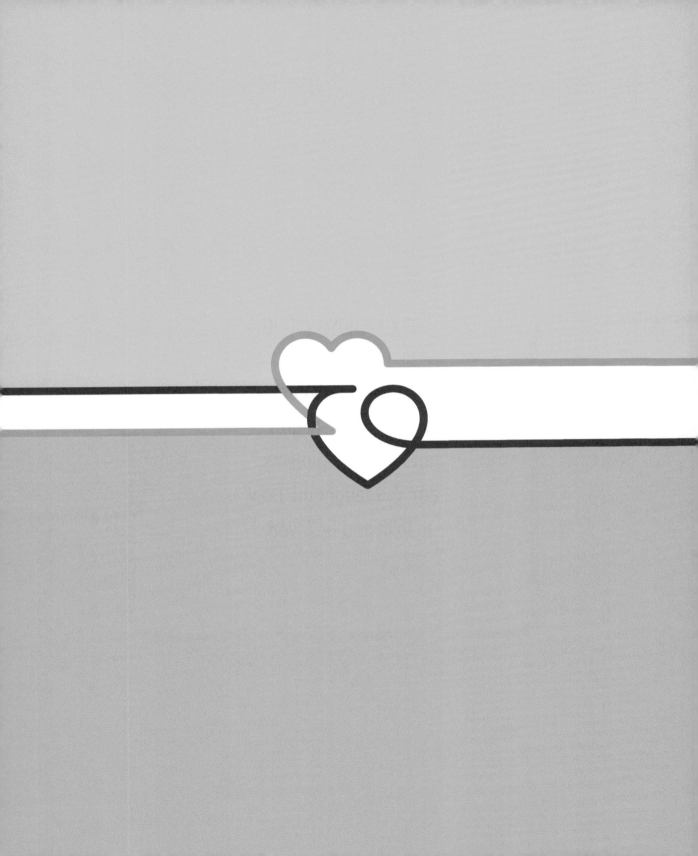

CONTENTS

INTRODUCTION

I started off as a family therapist at age twenty-two, working in New York City's child welfare system after graduate school. It was like being thrown in the deep end, and yet, having just come from an internship at Rikers Island jail, I thought to myself: *How much harder could it be?* I soon found out that "hard" didn't accurately describe what I would be faced with during the next seven years. As I supported families in crisis and supervised other therapists, I was given the opportunity to witness just how powerful love can be within a relationship. What I observed time and time again was that love can move mountains. Love can elicit our darkest emotions and can also propel us toward change in the most profound ways—all to maintain the bonds we hold dearest.

Working with families drew me to delve deeper into couples work in my own private practice. When two people feel supported and cared for by each other, when they create a safe haven within their relationship, freedom and authenticity can thrive. We can contain the deepest wounds, and yet, the existence of love between two people creates hope that things can be different and better. Love makes anything possible.

We also know that relationships take time, effort, and patience to thrive. In keeping with this reality, I set out to create something that would concretize the effort it takes to build a deep connection between two people. This book was born from countless hours witnessing and experiencing couples build intimacy, foster deep connections, overcome breakdowns, and regain trust—in my private practice, in my personal life, and within my own relationships. It is my hope that these activities will help you address some of the difficulties that arise during your daily life as a couple and enhance the connections you are fostering, regardless of what stage your relationship is in. We also acknowledge that this book is grounded in a monogamist framework and support other forms of relationship configurations as valid.

While this book is a wonderful way to work through complicated feelings, any ongoing or debilitating emotions should be addressed by a medical professional. There is no shame, only strength, in reaching out for support.

HOW TO USE THIS BOOK

The content in this book comes from a combination of theoretical training, direct clinical practice, lived personal experiences, and the experiences of my loved ones, which I've parlayed into creative, tangible exercises that are grounded in helping two people build a strong foundation.

The workbook is organized into thirteen chapters with five dynamic off-the-page activities within each. You may use this book however you wish. It's meant to be flexible and fit your needs, with no pressure to go from start to finish. My hope is that you use this workbook to create your own rituals that will enhance the time you spend together as a couple, especially if you find yourself too deep in the dreaded "Netflix and chill" monotony and craving more intentionality during your connecting time. Feel free to flip around to the activities that best suit your mood, take breaks on busy weeks, or tackle multiple activities in one sitting. Revisit any activity whenever you like.

Most of the supplies you'll need for the activities throughout the book are everyday things you may already have in your home, such as paper, writing utensils, basic art supplies, and a smartphone. Other materials you may need to acquire, such as food and beverage items. You'll find it helpful to keep the basic materials easily accessible, especially writing tools and scrap paper, so you can jump into an activity whenever you want.

Let this book work *for* you, not the other way around. I suggest each partner use a separate notebook, both to complete some of the activities and to memorialize your unique experience using this book. Remember that these activities are meant to be fun and thought-provoking and to provide you an opportunity to intentionally come together as a couple. I encourage you both to use the time working through this book to enjoy each other's company, learn about yourselves, learn each other's needs, and reflect on what makes your relationship truly special.

CHAPTER ONE

DEFINING LOVE IN RELATIONSHIPS

TRYING TO DEFINE a complex and amorphous concept such as love can feel nearly impossible. First off, love can mean many different things to different people. We can experience vastly different types of love depending on the relationship we find ourselves in. In fact, love can look and feel like something entirely different from each person's perspective *within* a single couple. To make things even more complicated, in our romantic relationship, the type of love we feel for each other can shift and change as the relationship moves through different stages. Because of this, it's no wonder many couples encounter all different types of conflicts related to showing and receiving love throughout the course of their relationship. The activities in this chapter are meant to help both of you define what love means in *your* relationship. Knowing what love means, feels, and looks like in your special and unique relationship can get you and your partner on the same page for relating to each other and sharing your expectations for each other and yourself, as well as guide you toward showing the type of love that you both crave.

WHAT IS LOVE?

Estimated time: **10 MINUTES**

Understanding love requires us to reflect on what it means to us, which helps us learn more about how we experience love as individuals. Before we can give love to another, we must first understand how we feel and experience love within ourselves. When we understand what love feels like for us, we can create a shared value system around love for our relationship. This will help both partners get and give the love you each deserve.

INSTRUCTIONS

1. Each partner writes down the words and phrases that come to mind when you think about love for the next three minutes. Feel free to draw pictures, share memories, and make references to art and media. The choice is yours. There are no wrong answers.

2. After three minutes, look over your papers together and underline where you see the same words or phrases. This is the start of your shared value system around love.

3. Take a look at what your partner wrote once more. Is there anything you'd like some additional clarification on? Ask your partner to elaborate.

LET'S TALK ABOUT IT

What did you notice when you compared what you each had written or drawn? Are there any overarching themes or major differences? Is there anything you learned about how you both see love? This discussion is a first step toward building a shared meaning for love in your relationship.

WHAT LOVE ISN'T

Estimated time: **10 MINUTES**

Society often shows us many examples of what love looks like, but what about the other side of the coin? How do we know what love *isn't*? What does it look like for you, specifically, when there's an absence of love? Knowing what love *isn't* can clue us in to where the gaps have been in our past relationships, which will set us up to know what we need in our current relationship.

INSTRUCTIONS

1. For the next three minutes, each partner writes down all the ways you have felt or witnessed an absence of love. How did you know love wasn't present? What did it feel and look like, in both your body and mind? (If you've experienced trauma related to love, big emotions may come up for you. Take a break as needed or take calming breaths as you do this exercise.)

2. After three minutes, share with each other and look for commonalities and differences. Underline common themes. Ask questions to better understand the areas you need clarification on or have curiosities around.

LET'S TALK ABOUT IT

What did you notice when you compared what you both had written? What were the themes, commonalities, and differences? Did you learn anything new or interesting about your partner? Thinking about what we don't want our love to look like will get us closer to what we do.

A DAY OF LOVE

Estimated time: **15 MINUTES**

Setting specific expectations for how we want to receive love can be incredibly helpful for both our partner and ourselves. It limits the guesswork and misunderstandings that can result in a lot of frustration on both ends. We often get into the trap of thinking our partners should know what we need, but it's important to remember that none of us can read minds! This activity will help both of you get a sense of what an ideal day of love would look like so that your partner can be clued in to how often, how much, and what types of love you most prefer. For this activity, ask yourself, "What would my ideal day of love look like?"

> **SUPPLIES**
>
> Two notebooks/ scrap paper or calendar (paper or digital)
>
> Two writing utensils

INSTRUCTIONS

1. Each partner separately writes out a time schedule from the time you wake up to the time you go to sleep. Imagine that the schedule is for one day in which you get the perfect amount and preferred types of love. (You'll find an example on page 5.)

2. Add one or two activities to your schedule that you would like to do *with* your partner.

3. Add one or two activities to your schedule that you would like to do *for* your partner.

4. Add one or two activities to your schedule that you would like your partner to do *for* you.

5. These activities should reflect *your* ideal day of love. (You can even include time apart if that would help you feel love for your partner.)

6. When you both have finished planning out your ideal day, take turns sharing your schedules with each other and allow for questions from your partner to better understand.

7. Let each other know if you're willing to do the activities listed on your partner's ideal love day.

8. If there are any activities listed that you wouldn't be willing to try out, give an alternative suggestion to your partner.

9. Plan two days within the next month to try each of your love schedules and see how it goes.

EXAMPLE

8:00 a.m. Partner wakes me up with coffee.

10:00 a.m. Work out alone.

1:00 p.m. I check in by sending a funny meme.

7:00 p.m. I cook; we eat dinner together.

8:00 p.m. Partner does a load of laundry.

10:00 p.m. We go to bed together and chat before falling asleep.

LET'S TALK ABOUT IT
What did you notice about the types, amount, and timing of the love you desire versus what your partner wants? Where did you overlap, and where did you have different expectations? Understanding each other's expectations is an important step in a relationship. Proactively communicating our needs can set us up to get the love we deserve and can also prevent fights that occur due to a lack of clarity about each other's expectations.

MANUAL FOR LOVING ME

Estimated time: **25 TO 30 MINUTES**

Humans are unique individuals with specific needs, quirks, pet peeves, and ways of interacting. Wouldn't it be nice if you could exchange manuals that outlined this information? The result would be fewer surprises, as you'd have a helpful guide to refer to when things get tricky! If you could create a user-friendly manual to help your partner in caring for you, what sorts of things would it include? Creating your very own user manual will not only help your partner but will also help you reflect on your specific preferences and build your ability to explicitly state your needs. Remember to have fun and make it your own. Be as concrete, abstract, or silly as you like. You might even turn this into a recipe with "cooking" instructions!

> **SUPPLIES**
>
> Two notebooks or scrap paper
>
> Favorite writing and drawing utensils

INSTRUCTIONS

1. Each partner begins their own manual with an "Elements" section, outlining the parts that make you fundamentally you. Maybe you have a passion for travel, require daily back rubs, and enjoy witty banter. Instead, maybe you'd rather outline your core values in this section such as spirituality, loyalty, and humor. (You'll find an example on page 7.)

2. Next, write your "Usage" instructions. This section will help ensure your partner's success in loving or caring for you. What areas should your partner be aware of on a regular basis?

3. Now write your "Safety" instructions. These are the important precautions your partner should or should not take when interacting with you. Maybe you get cranky when you're hungry. Let your partner know this. (Add drawings or emoticons to illustrate your moods.)

4. Add a "FAQ" section as a reference guide to commonly asked questions. What else do you think your partner should know about being with you?

5. When finished, share your manuals with each other.

EXAMPLE

Elements

2 tbsp of travel

3 cups of emotion connection

1 dash of dark humor

Usage Instructions

One thing that de-stresses me is _____ .

I need _____ and _____ to function.

Safety Instructions

Nothing makes me angrier than when _____ .

You'll know I've hit my capacity when _____ .

FAQs

Q: How often do you like to see family?

A: Biweekly

Q: What is your least favorite chore?

A: Taking out the trash

LET'S TALK ABOUT IT

What did you learn about your partner? Discuss when you might refer to these manuals and what you might add as time goes on. This will increase your comfort with proactively speaking your needs while setting realistic expectations.

LOVE YOURSELF FIRST

Estimated time: **1 DAY**

We sometimes forget that the best way to love others is to focus on loving ourselves first. Loving ourselves can be difficult if we often say harsh or nasty things to ourselves. Thankfully, put-downs and self-criticism are learned behaviors, meaning we can also unlearn them through practicing positive self-talk. When we're depleted, which can often come from being highly self-critical, it can feel nearly impossible to give our loved ones the support and care they require. When we say kind and helpful things to ourselves, it becomes easier and more realistic for us to say these things to another.

SUPPLIES

Separate notebooks

Writing utensils

INSTRUCTIONS

1. Together, read through the list of positive affirmations on page 9.

2. Each partner copies them on a separate piece of paper.

3. Put an asterisk next to the phrases that you have an easy time believing, underline the phrases you could believe with practice, and circle the ones you don't believe at all. As you start to practice positive self-talk separately, you'll begin by repeating the phrases you have an easier time believing, working up to the ones that are harder to internalize.

4. Over the next day, practice writing, speaking, and saying these phrases out loud or silently. You can say them randomly or say them whenever you hear yourself getting self-critical. In those moments, interrupt yourself and replace your negative thought with one of the phrases on page 9.

5. Keep your notebook nearby and jot down any thoughts or feelings that come to mind as you go about your day.

6. Check in with your partner at the end of the day to see your results.

Positive Affirmations

I love myself.

I am enough.

I am worthy of love.

I am capable.

I am smart.

I deserve what I seek.

I bring others joy.

I am not a burden.

I am a good and kind person.

I am beautiful.

LET'S TALK ABOUT IT
What was easy or difficult about practicing positive self-talk?
What did you notice about the phrases that were hardest
for you? How did repeating these phrases impact behaviors
throughout your day? Did it impact your relationship? If so,
share how with your partner. Think through and discuss how
you could make this a regular practice in which you hold each
other accountable.

CHAPTER TWO

TRUST IS A CHOICE

TRUST IS ONE of the foundational pillars that make our relationships strong or resistant to breakdowns. It is the key to growing your relationship into a partnership that you both want. Without trust, a relationship may be destined to stay stagnant, break down, or feel unsatisfying. Although, as with love, people experience trust in different ways, trust is generally comprised of a sense of safety, security, and reliance on each other. Without trust, it can feel nearly impossible to make decisions, express vulnerability, and overcome impasses in our relationships. We all need something stable to stand on in order to experience the emotional safety required to take risks, express our needs, and love each other fully. Trust is not something you achieve in a relationship and then never need to work on again. Building and maintaining trust requires choosing to put in the work on a regular basis. This may include frequent check-ins, attuning to our partner's daily needs, and determining what adjustments are needed to sustain progress. The activities in this chapter will help both of you tap into what you need to build and sustain trust as well as help you avoid potential pitfalls that result in the breakdown of trust.

SQUARE UP

Estimated time: **10 MINUTES**

Trusting our partner can feel like a terrifying leap of faith; however, to build a strong foundation, both people must take that risk. To build trust, learning to depend on each other for support is important. Completing a task together blindfolded is a fun way to practice effective communication and collaboration. This activity will help you practice depending on each other's insights and input when you both are at a disadvantage.

SUPPLIES

Blindfolds

Rope

INSTRUCTIONS

1. Start in a standing position.

2. Face each other blindfolded while holding the rope together.

3. Drop the rope at the same time on the count of three.

4. Take three steps away from where you dropped the rope.

5. Return to the rope and work together to lay the rope out in a perfect square.

6. Take off your blindfolds and look at the result together.

LET'S TALK ABOUT IT

What roles did you both gravitate toward? How difficult was it to not have your sense of sight and instead rely on each other? When we're at a disadvantage, it's easy to be afraid and unsure; however, these are the moments when you can help each other pick up the slack.

LET THE BIDDING BEGIN!

Estimated time: **15 MINUTES**

Trust increases in relationships when partners meet each other's requests, or bids, for connection. Bids can include asking for attention, affection, or intimacy from our partner. Partners have three options when a bid for connection is made: turn toward by meeting the need, do nothing, or turn against by attacking, defending, or saying no.

SUPPLIES

When your partner turns toward you, not only does your need get met, but you also learn that you can trust your partner to give support when needed. In daily life, this is easier said than done. It's common to miss our partner's bids for connection when we're stressed or busy. When we miss a bid, this is us "doing nothing." Although it's not as destructive as turning against, it leaves our partner unsure about where we stand. Conversely, when a partner often turns against your requests by defending or attacking, reaching out for support may begin to feel unsafe. This exercise will help both of you recognize each other's bids for connection by turning toward them more often, building a foundation for trust.

INSTRUCTIONS

1. One person starts by communicating a feeling. You may want to use this formula:

   "I feel _____ when _____." (These are called impact statements.)

2. The other person's role is to listen, face their partner and look at them, disregarding distractions and emotionally putting themselves in their partner's shoes.

3. When your partner is done speaking, resist rushing to offer solutions and instead communicate that you heard their message and that the causes of these feelings are understood. In essence, you're saying "I hear you."

4. Switch positions and repeat.

LET'S TALK ABOUT IT

What went well during this activity? Do you have any constructive feedback for your partner about their ability to turn toward you? Discuss different ways you feel supported so your partner can practice the various ways to turn toward you. Notice the differences in how you two prefer to be turned toward. Recognizing your partner's bids for connections more often than not will build trust that you can be vulnerable around each other and be there to offer support.

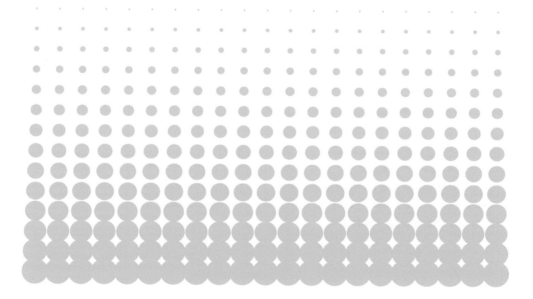

TRUST BANK ACCOUNT

Estimated time: **1 DAY**

Trust is built in our everyday moments of life, not in the grand, sweeping gestures or promises made. Think about your relationship as having two trust bank accounts, one for each of you. When you do something that builds trust for your partner, you're putting a deposit into their bank account. When you do something dishonest or harmful to your relationship, you're withdrawing from your partner's bank account. The same concept applies to your own bank account and your partner's actions. The aim of this activity is to help balance your bank accounts, with more deposits than withdrawals, as well as to practice noticing little moments that build or break down trust in each other. (You'll see an example on page 15.)

SUPPLIES

Separate notebooks, writing utensils

INSTRUCTIONS

1. In your separate notebooks, make two columns, one with the heading "Deposits" (for behaviors that make deposits in your bank account) and the other "Withdrawals" (for behaviors that make withdrawals in your bank account). Write down all the things you can think of that personally build and diminish trust for you.

2. Share your lists with your partner and ask any clarifying questions. Refrain from using this as an opportunity to critique your partner's list. Accept the list as it is.

3. Over the next day, take note of your bank account's deposits and withdrawals.

4. Discuss how the day went at the end of your day. Remember: The objective is not to blame each other for wrongdoing, but instead to get a sense of how balanced your bank accounts are. Look for areas that need rebalancing and discuss them as a couple.

DEPOSITS	WITHDRAWALS
Example	Example
1. Compliments	1. Put-downs or making fun of me
2. Following through with the plan we made	2. Excessively canceling plans

LET'S TALK ABOUT IT

How does it feel to think about trust in this way? What do you notice about what is on your lists versus your partner's? You may notice as you went through the day that you were more aware of your actions as well, considering what behaviors you do that might be making deposits or taking out withdrawals. This activity helps you both increase awareness around the little moments that build and break down trust.

SHARING PAST BETRAYALS

Estimated time: **25 MINUTES**

Similar to understanding love, knowing what trust feels like requires us to reflect on difficult times when our trust was broken down or lost completely. Although remembering tough times can be painful, it can help our partner learn what's required for us to feel emotionally safe in our relationship. Sharing past betrayals not only builds a deeper connection with our partner, but it can also guide us to proactively plan together so similar issues don't arise in the future. When you are aware of our past betrayals, you can gain a better understanding around why certain things are upsetting or scary. What may originally look like an over-reaction will suddenly make sense when you understand your partner's past experiences within a larger context.

> **SUPPLIES**
>
> Separate notebooks, writing utensils

INSTRUCTIONS

1. Think back to a past relationship that ended in a betrayal. What caused it? How did it make you feel? What did you learn from that experience? Write freely for the next ten minutes. Write what you feel comfortable sharing.

2. Take turns sharing your writing with each other.

3. If comfortable, allow your partner to ask questions about your experience. Communicate care and understanding for each other.

4. Write down some agreements on a separate sheet of paper that would help you guard against experiencing something similar in the future. (Remember to only focus on what is in your control, which is different than blaming yourself for what happened to you.)

5. This may have brought up some difficult emotions and bad memories. End with a ten-second hug to finish the exercise, leaving you both in an emotionally safer place.

LET'S TALK ABOUT IT

How was it to share such a vulnerable topic with your partner? How was it to hear about your partner's difficult past? Where do you spot commonalities? This is an opportunity to build a shared value system around trust so that you both know where you stand and how to minimize instances of hurting each other. Unfortunately, it's impossible to completely guard against hurting each other. But if we know our loved one's major pain points, we can do our very best to avoid them.

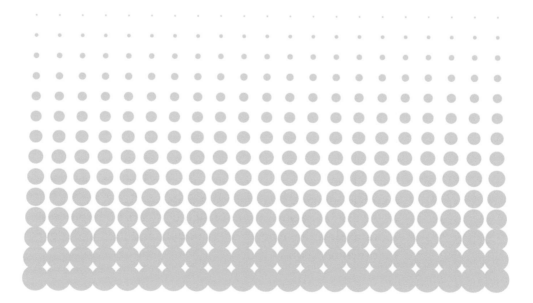

ACTIVE LISTENING

Estimated time: **10 MINUTES**

Active listening is the practice of deeply listening in order to create mutual understanding, which helps both partners feel heard and respected. This can be extremely difficult in the age of social media and addictive internet games. It's easier than ever to divide your attention, which can have consequences for building trust. Failing to actively listen won't immediately make or break the trust you've built, but it can build up resentments, especially if either or both of you continue to feel unheard or misunderstood.

<table>
<tr><td>SUPPLIES

Two notebooks and writing utensils or whiteboard and markers

Timer</td></tr>
</table>

INSTRUCTIONS

1. For thirty seconds, tell your partner about something that recently happened to you.

2. Your partner listens intently and writes down any important phrases or feelings they heard. (Remember to face each other, maintain eye contact, and minimize distractions.)

3. Once you finish, your partner summarizes what they heard, also known as "reflecting back." They begin by stating, "What I hear you saying is . . ." and communicate what they heard, using their own words.

4. When your partner reflects back, clarify anything that was missed or misunderstood.

5. Switch positions and repeat the steps.

LET'S TALK ABOUT IT
Which position was easier for you? Was it difficult to simply reflect back instead of jump in with your own thoughts? We are often eager to respond immediately with our opinions, which can leave our partner feeling unheard. It's important for us to slow down and seek to understand their experience before moving on.

CHAPTER THREE

EXPLORING THE LANGUAGES OF LOVE

HUMANS EXPERIENCE LOVE in their own unique and individual ways. Building on this premise, relationship expert Dr. Gary Chapman developed the popular concept of love languages, which says that there are five distinct ways of expressing and receiving love. Dr. Chapman believed that each of us prefers to show and receive love differently. The five love languages include words of affirmation, quality time, gifts, acts of service, and physical touch. As you work through this chapter, you may find that you prefer "speaking" some of these languages more often than others. Identifying your personal love preferences as well as those of your loved ones will help you more deeply connect and build intimacy with each other. Learning to recognize specific and individual preferences in a relationship can help prevent conflicts from arising when needs have been misunderstood or gone unmet. The activities in this chapter will help you discover your primary love language(s), test how well you know your partner's, and get you into the habit of using what you've learned to relate to and interact with each other as your relationship develops.

LEARNING THE LOVE LANGUAGES

Estimated time: **5 MINUTES**

Many partners come to their relationship believing there are only one or two behaviors that express their love. It can take some time to fully grasp there are multiple ways—or languages—to show and receive love. The purpose of this activity is to increase your understanding of each love language. When you understand love languages, you'll start noticing them in your daily life.

SUPPLIES
———
Two pieces of scrap paper, two writing utensils

INSTRUCTIONS

1. One person reads the first love ask from page 21. On separate sheets of paper, both of you write down the love language that matches the ask.

2. The other person reads the second love ask. You each, again, write down the corresponding love language.

3. Switching positions as in steps 1 and 2, move through the rest of the Love Asks list.

4. Compare answers. Tally how many answers you got right. (You'll find an answer key at the bottom of page 21.) Discuss what feelings become present for you.

LOVE ASKS	**LOVE LANGUAGES**

LOVE ASKS

1. Tell me I look attractive in a certain article of clothing.

2. Do my least favorite chore.

3. Buy me a small token of affection.

4. Go for a walk with me.

5. Give me a hug.

6. Write me a loving text.

7. Ask me what you can do to help lighten my load.

8. Tell me why you like me.

9. Buy me something I've had my eye on.

10. Give me a shoulder massage.

LOVE LANGUAGES

a. *Words of Affirmation*

b. *Quality Time*

c. *Acts of Service*

d. *Physical Touch*

e. *Gifts*

LET'S TALK ABOUT IT

Were any of the statements difficult to categorize? Have you thought of love in these ways before? How does it help you think about your relationship in a new way? When we expand our idea of what love is, we can try new ways of relating to each other.

ANSWER KEY: 1. a; 2. c; 3. e; 4. b; 5. d; 6. a; 7. c; 8. a; 9. e; 10. d

WOULD YOU RATHER?

Estimated time: **10 MINUTES**

Now that you have a better understanding of what each love language is, it's time to think about what your preferred love languages are. Knowing the ways that we prefer to receive love will help us communicate our needs. We also need our partners to do the same to be able to continue learning how to care for them.

SUPPLIES

Two notebooks or scrap paper

Two writing utensils

INSTRUCTIONS

1. Read each "would you rather" question.

2. Use the Notebook List on the following page as your guide.

3. Review your lists together to see which love language(s) you chose most often.

WOULD YOU RATHER . . .

1. . . . watch a **movie** or receive a **back massage**?

2. . . . **travel** together or receive an expensive **gift**?

3. . . . hear **"I love you"** or have me cross an item off your **to-do list**?

4. . . . go out for a **date** or receive a **love letter**?

5. . . . **hold hands** or receive a **token of affection**?

6. . . . have an interesting **conversation** or be **snuggled**?

7. . . . have me do a **chore** or be told why you're **lovable**?

8. . . . be told **"I'm proud of you"** or receive **help** for a task?

9. . . . **make out** or go on an **adventure**?

10. . . . receive a special **surprise** or get support on a **project**?

| | | **NOTEBOOK LIST** |

Partner 1   **Partner 2**

Partner 1	Partner 2	
——————	——————	**1.** Quality Time or Physical Touch
——————	——————	**2.** Quality Time or Gifts
——————	——————	**3.** Words of Affirmation or Acts of Service
——————	——————	**4.** Quality Time or Words of Affirmation
——————	——————	**5.** Physical Touch or Gifts
——————	——————	**6.** Quality Time or Physical Touch
——————	——————	**7.** Acts of Service or Words of Affirmation
——————	——————	**8.** Words of Affirmation or Acts of Service
——————	——————	**9.** Physical Touch or Quality Time
——————	——————	**10.** Gifts or Acts of Service

LET'S TALK ABOUT IT

Which love language(s) did you gravitate toward? Did anything surprise you about your answers? You're learning more about how you and your partner like to be loved. Take note and use what you've learned!

LOVE LANGUAGES: NEWLYWED STYLE

Estimated time: **15 MINUTES**

Let's go deeper and apply what you have learned about love languages to see how well you know each other's preferences. It's natural to enjoy multiple types of love languages and enjoy some more than others. This is an opportunity for you to rank your love languages and make some guesses about how your partner would rank theirs. Let's see how well you know each other and what more you need to learn! When we can anticipate each other's needs, we build trust and safety in our relationship. It feels great to have our partner see us for who we are by giving us what we need to feel loved.

> **SUPPLIES**
>
> Note cards
> ———
> Two writing utensils

INSTRUCTIONS

1. Together, read the first sentence in the table at right.

2. Separately, write on your note card the number you think your partner would rank that statement as, with one being least important and five being most important.

3. Put your note card facedown so your partner can't see your answer.

4. On the count of three, each flip your note card to reveal your ranking! Notice if the rankings mismatch.

5. Use a new note card for the next sentence and begin the process again until you reach the last sentence.

I love it when you kiss me deeply.

———

I love it when you make our shared space nicer.

———

I love it when you buy me a thoughtful present.

———

I love it when you give me an unsolicited compliment.

———

I love it when we spend time together without distractions.

———

LET'S TALK ABOUT IT

What do you notice about the statements that are most important to you? Where do you and your partner relate and differ? Whether you've been together for weeks or years, it's never too soon or too late to check in around how we feel most loved as a helpful way to reconnect and recalibrate!

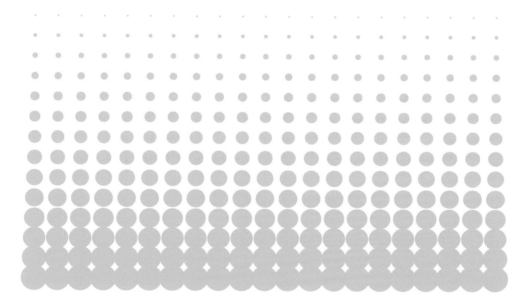

PRACTICING DIRECT REQUESTS

Estimated time: **20 MINUTES**

We tend to give the type of love we want to receive from our partner as a way of dropping hints for how to love us. What would it be like instead to directly *ask* our partner for the exact type of love we desire? If you're thinking this sounds scary or vulnerable, you're right! It is. Just because we're in a committed relationship doesn't mean it's always easy to ask for what we want. We may fear we'll be rejected or ignored. This activity will help you increase your comfort about asking for the type of love you desire in a way that is both motivating to your partner and sets them up for success.

> **SUPPLIES**
>
> none

INSTRUCTIONS

1. Face each other and ignore distractions while making eye contact.

2. One person completes the sentence: "I feel most cared for when you _____." In the blank, offer a concrete example of your preferred love language.

   (Notice that this statement is phrased in the positive, not negative. Phrasing requests in the positive is more motivating for our partner than starting with "You never . . . " or "How come you don't . . .")

3. The other person responds by asking exploratory, open-ended questions. Think: Who, what, when, where, why, and how? If your partner communicates that they like compliments, what questions do you have to better understand what type, how often, and when? Maybe your partner likes compliments about their intellect instead of their physicality. What might you ask to figure that out?

4. Once the second person understands the request, communicate whether you're willing to comply with the request. If you are unable to meet the request, explain why and offer an alternative solution. Your partner can either accept or suggest an alternative until the need is agreed upon by both of you.

5. Switch positions and repeat.

LET'S TALK ABOUT IT

How was it to ask so directly for what you need? Have either of you gotten into the trap of thinking your partner should already know? It's important to remember our partner can rarely, if ever, read our minds. Being up front about the love we crave and allowing room for questions will help minimize conflicts and lead to a better understanding of our needs and abilities to satisfy those needs.

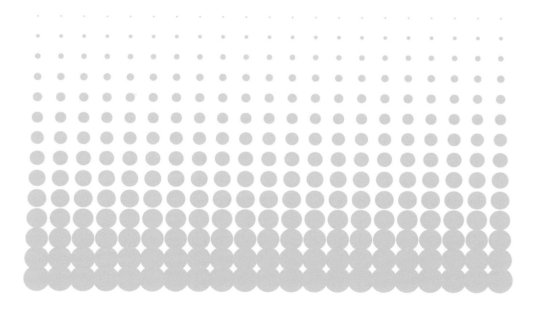

OUR LOVE LANGUAGE CALENDAR

Estimated time: **30 MINUTES**

Learning about love languages is only useful if we put what we have learned into practice on a regular basis. Now that you both have a better idea of which love languages you gravitate toward, it's time to sit down together and intentionally plan out when, where, and how you're going to show each other the love you both desire. This is a great time to get creative and practice specificity around asking for our needs. When we are specific, our partner has a much better chance of satisfying our desires for love and affection.

INSTRUCTIONS

1. Use scrap paper or a whiteboard to each sketch out a two-week calendar. Fill out the dates for the next two weeks.

2. Discuss the types of love languages that you want to prioritize for the next two weeks. Pick two love languages for each of you.

3. Add any major personal and professional obligations to your calendar to understand where your capacities are. This will allow you to plan realistically based on your actual scheduled responsibilities.

4. Add activities to your calendar that will satisfy your partner's love languages. One person writes down activities in their calendar to show love to their partner, and vice versa. (For example: If you both love quality time, plan a date night and add it to both calendars. If one person loves acts of service, the other person can plan an activity that would satisfy that need.)

5. Share what you've planned and ask for feedback and adjustments. If your partner's plan requires you to be present, copy those plans into your own calendar so you are ready to receive that love.

LET'S TALK ABOUT IT

How did it feel to think through specific ways that you were going to show each other love? What was most difficult about putting love languages into practice? It's one thing to know what type of love we desire but quite another to figure out how we are going to apply this learning to our daily lives. When we intentionally plan in our relationship, we know what to expect and have a better chance of getting what we need from each other.

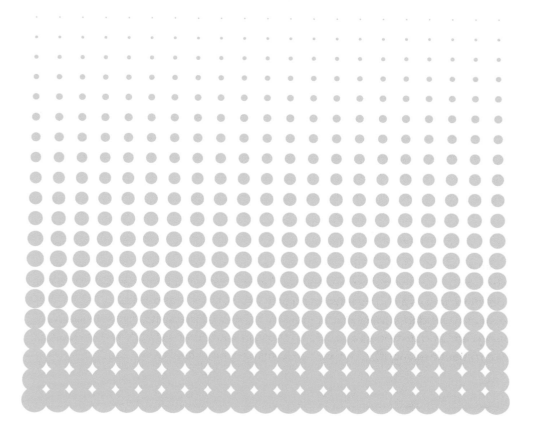

CHAPTER FOUR

MAINTAINING SOCIAL CIRCLES

FINDING SOMEONE YOU connect with romantically can be incredibly fulfilling and transformational; however, it's important to stay mindful of other relationships, too. Cultivating and maintaining different types of relationships is important for feeling more joy, comfort, and satisfaction in your life. Although you may try, it's impossible for your romantic partner to meet all your needs. In fact, putting pressure on your relationship to constantly satisfy all your needs can be detrimental to your individual mental health and to the well-being of your partnership. Healthy relationships require the creation and maintenance of outer social circles to preserve individual identities outside the relationship. Spending time apart with others also gives the necessary space to check in with your own needs and desires. Spending time as a couple interacting with family, friends, and colleagues can also serve as a wonderful way to bring more depth and richness into your relationship. Being seen and treated as a couple by those in your outer network adds meaning to your romantic relationship, which builds intimacy and stability.

FRIENDSHIP INVENTORY

Estimated time: **15 MINUTES**

When we set out to cultivate and maintain social circles outside our relationship, it's helpful to take an inventory of the people currently in our life and how we experience those relationships. This activity will help you reflect on the relationships you have and think critically and intentionally about your desired frequency of interaction. It will also help you think through if you're getting as much as you give to those relationships.

INSTRUCTIONS

1. Each uses your separate notebook to write down a list of people outside your relationship. Add everyone you can think of whom you interact with on a regular to semi-regular basis: family, friends, acquaintances, colleagues.

2. Next to their name, note how often you interact with each person (weekly, biweekly, monthly, every season, etc.).

3. Write down how often you'd *like* to interact with them.

4. Write down what you get from this relationship (emotional support, a dancing partner, etc.).

5. Write down what you give to this relationship.

6. Share your list with your partner.

LET'S TALK ABOUT IT
What thoughts and feelings came up for you as you did this activity? This exercise is a great way to reflect on our outside relationships and ask ourselves: Do we have the type of relationship we desire and, if not, what do we need to cultivate a connection that better suits our needs?

SPENDING TIME APART

Estimated time: **20 MINUTES**

Spending time apart from your romantic relationship can feel vastly different to each partner, for a variety of reasons, including but not limited to how long you've have been together, expectations you have for each other, how you were raised, and any leftover emotional baggage from past relationships. Depending on these factors, getting away from each other can feel comfortable and safe, very scary and destabilizing, or a combination of all. Knowing this, it's imperative for partners in romantic relationships to tolerate a certain amount of space to promote individual senses of self and maintain other important relationships. Without the ability to safely separate from each other when needed, there's no opportunity to build a bridge and connect again.

> **SUPPLIES**
>
> Two notebooks or scrap paper
>
> Two writing utensils

INSTRUCTIONS

1. Take turns asking each other the interview questions in step 3.

2. Practice active listening and deep, slow breathing while asking and answering, as feelings may get triggered, depending on how comfortable you feel having time away from loved ones. Remember: You are not trying to solve anything. You're only trying to better understand each other's desires and expectations about spending time apart while seeing others.

3. As you listen to your partner's answers, take notes of any important information you want to remember.

   • Ideally, how often would you like to spend time apart spending time with others?

   • How would you like to communicate to me that you need space to do so?

- How would you like me to communicate to you that I need space?

- What activities do you want to do by yourself with others?

- What would it look like if one of us wanted space but the other didn't?

- What would you need to feel safe and confident about spending time apart?

LET'S TALK ABOUT IT

What was helpful and what was hard about that conversation? What did you learn about your partner's needs? Did you learn anything about your own need for space? Having productive and safe conversations about our desires to spend time with others is just as important as the actual spending time with others because it shows us that our relationship can plan for space without breaking down or leading to dysfunction.

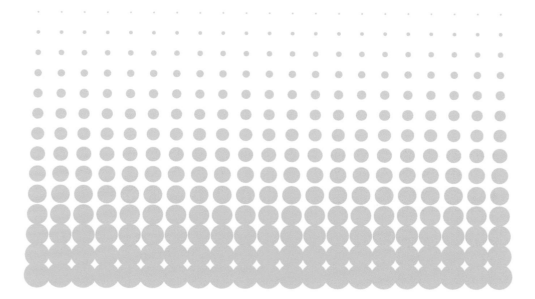

PLATONIC LOVE LETTER

Estimated time: **20 MINUTES**

While love letters are most common in romantic relationships, it's just as important to let friends know that not only are they loved but also *why* they are loved. Friends are sometimes the first people to demonstrate love after parents and caregivers. While we expect that parents and caregivers will provide love, the decision to love a friend is a choice. Sometimes, your friendships are your longest relationships, even longer than the relationship you have with the partner you've come to care deeply for. Taking some time to shower your friends with love helps deepen your outside relationships and helps you and your partner reflect on the different types of love you each have in your lives.

> **SUPPLIES**
>
> Construction paper
>
> Markers or pens
>
> Two envelopes
>
> Two postage stamps

INSTRUCTIONS

1. Both partners spend ten to fifteen minutes writing a love letter, each to your closest friend. While you both write, reflect on your friendship history, fun memories, difficult but important experiences, and what this relationship has meant to you. Tell your friend in your letter why you care for them.

2. After both of you have finished writing, spend the next ten minutes decorating your love letters. Feel free to get as creative as you like, and use any art supplies that inspire you!

3. When finished decorating, if comfortable, each read your letter aloud to your partner.

4. While you read, the listening partner should practice active listening by not interrupting and minimizing distractions. This is not a time for the listening partner to ask questions or give feedback. The letters you both have written are perfect as they are.

5. When the speaking partner is finished sharing, the listening partner thanks the speaking partner for sharing something vulnerable and meaningful about their friendship.

6. Address both letters to your chosen friends and mail them.

LET'S TALK ABOUT IT

What was the process of writing your letter like? What thoughts and emotions came up for you? How did it feel to hear what your partner loves about their friendship? How did you feel sitting in silence decorating your letter alongside your partner? Spending time in silence doing something creative is especially stress-relieving for our relationships, and it's a nice way to remain connected with our partner while also putting in effort with our outside social circle.

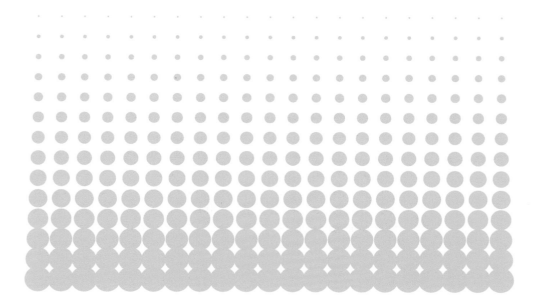

FRIENDLY TEMPERATURE CHECK

Estimated time: **20 MINUTES**

SUPPLIES

Two notebooks
or scrap paper

Writing utensils

Many of us have experienced a friend starting a new relationship and temporarily forgetting about their friendship with us. In fact, you may have also been the friend who momentarily forgets about your friendships as you focus on your new and exciting relationship. This period in romantic relationships is called the limerence phase. It can be frustrating for friends as they wait it out, hoping you'll return to them when the big, intense feelings subside as you begin to feel more stable in the romantic partnership. Regardless of what phase your relationship is in, this activity will help you both proactively reflect on your friendships, see where you need to adjust, and create a plan for moving forward.

INSTRUCTIONS

1. You each select one close friend to do the temperature check on.

2. Review each statement and rate yourself on the scale using your notebooks.

3. Notice what areas require some improvement by seeing where you marked "Disagree" or "Strongly Disagree."

4. Make plans to work on the area that you scored lower on. Share your plan with your partner as added accountability.

LET'S TALK ABOUT IT

What did you notice about the areas you agreed with versus the areas you disagreed with? What was it like doing this temperature check alongside your partner? A mark of a healthy and secure relationship is our ability to support and encourage our partner's friendships outside our relationship. Being accountable to each other can help you maintain your separate social circles while at the same time deepening your relationship as you support each other's goals.

A. I've initiated a hangout in the past month.

	Strongly Agree	Agree	Neutral	Disagree	Strongly Disagree
Partner 1	❏	❏	❏	❏	❏
Partner 2	❏	❏	❏	❏	❏

B. I've called or texted this friend in the past two weeks.

Partner 1	❏	❏	❏	❏	❏
Partner 2	❏	❏	❏	❏	❏

C. I generally know what's going on in their life.

Partner 1	❏	❏	❏	❏	❏
Partner 2	❏	❏	❏	❏	❏

D. When we recently spoke, I gave them my full attention.

Partner 1	❏	❏	❏	❏	❏
Partner 2	❏	❏	❏	❏	❏

E. When we spoke, there was a relatively equal split of sharing and listening.

Partner 1	❏	❏	❏	❏	❏
Partner 2	❏	❏	❏	❏	❏

GROUP DATE PLANNING

Estimated time: **15 MINUTES**

Going on a double or group date can be a fun and different way to experience your romantic relationship. The experience when it's just you two can look and feel vastly different than when you're interacting together with others. Double and group dates can give you more information about your partnership. Going out with others helps you maintain social circles and recognize specific needs related to interacting with your partner in a larger group. Use this activity to have some fun with your partner creating invitations for your date!

> **SUPPLIES**
>
> Two notebooks or scrap paper
>
> Two writing utensils
>
> Postcards
>
> Stickers (optional)
>
> Postage stamps

INSTRUCTIONS

1. Decide on a group date activity that you're both interested in. (Examples might include bowling, beach day, park picnic, hike, laser tag, day at the arcade, etc.)

2. Make a list of attendees.

3. Obtain their home addresses.

4. Buy postcards that represent the activity you'll be doing on your date. (Or create the theme with stickers.)

5. Write out invitations using postcards.

6. Mail your invites to your guests.

LET'S TALK ABOUT IT

How was it to spend time together planning out a group activity? When you were on the date, what did you notice about how you interacted as a couple versus when you're part of a larger group? What did you like about how you interacted when you were with a larger group? What would you change?

CHAPTER FIVE

NURTURING INTIMACY

INTIMACY IS DEFINED as closeness between two people that builds over time the more you get to know and trust each other. The experience of intimacy consists of vulnerability, openness, and the sharing of your authentic selves with each other. Building and nurturing intimacy in romantic relationships is imperative, as it allows for necessary and deeper bonding and connection with partners on multiple levels: physically, emotionally, and spiritually. All couples face a range of issues in the course of relationships; however, the presence of intimacy can allow both of you to overcome these issues with more ease, compassion, creativity, and understanding. When you know who your partner fundamentally is, and when you can allow yourself to be authentic with them, you can more easily surf the inevitable waves that come with being in love. The activities in this chapter will help you understand the level of intimacy that currently exists in your relationship, build more intimacy, and discover ways to nurture the intimacy that already exists between you two.

CREATING LOVE MAPS

Estimated time: **20 MINUTES**

SUPPLIES

Two pieces of
poster board

Markers

Drs. John and Julie Gottman, renowned couples' therapists, dubbed the process of getting to know your partner's internal world "building love maps." Love maps consists of each of your desires, memories, and fears, and your past, present, and future experiences. When we begin a new relationship, we know little about our partner's world; our main objective is to learn more. In doing so, we begin to fill out our partner's love map. Even if you've been together for many years, there's always more to learn and add to your partner's love map. When we add detail to our partner's love map, we build intimacy. The more information and nuance we add, the closer we become and the more perspective we gain when things get difficult.

INSTRUCTIONS

1. Each partner takes a poster board and draws their self-portrait. (No drawing skills are required. Use whatever style suits you.) Include qualities that you like about yourself, both outwardly and inwardly.

2. Then, at your head, each hand, and each foot, draw five big circles. These represent "domains": relationships, career, health, hobbies, purpose.

3. Inside each domain, draw pictures and symbols that reflect what is most important to you in that domain.

4. Present your picture to each other and explain what you've drawn.

LET'S TALK ABOUT IT
As you drew, did you gain any clarity about yourself? Did you learn anything new about your partner once they shared their picture? How did it impact your feelings of closeness? As time goes on, remember to add to your love maps to deepen your understanding of each other.

CATCH THEM DOING GOOD

Estimated time: **10 MINUTES**

We often try to motivate our partner by pointing out something they do that we don't appreciate. While it is important to speak up when we're mistreated or disappointed, it's equally important and more motivating when we point out when our partner *succeeds* at satisfying our needs. "Catching them doing good" in real time, by acknowledging their good behavior and showing appreciation, not only builds their confidence in caring for us but also strengthens our connection.

SUPPLIES

INSTRUCTIONS

1. Choose an everyday activity to complete together for the next ten minutes, such as doing laundry or washing/drying dishes.

2. As you complete this activity, practice communicating *only* in acknowledgments of the positive.

3. Take note of what your partner is doing well during this activity and point it out by saying it aloud.

4. If your partner does something you don't appreciate, instead of saying "Don't do it that way," try saying "I really appreciate it when you do it like this . . ." and show them.

5. When you're "catching them doing good," be careful not to end the acknowledgment sentence with "But I really wish you did it more!" Ending appreciation in a complaint ruins the positive impact.

LET'S TALK ABOUT IT

How did it feel to receive appreciation? How did it feel to communicate appreciation? Was it difficult to show only positive acknowledgment or to stop yourself from continuing with a "but"? Showing appreciation is one of the most powerful currencies we have in a relationship, yet it costs us nothing.

WHAT'S ON THE MENU?

Estimated time: **25 MINUTES**

Although popular media suggests that when you enter a sexual relationship, you should simply know what your partner likes and dislikes, rarely is this the case. Sharing desires with each other and seeing where your desires overlap will not only help build intimacy but will also result in a more enriching sexual relationship for both parties. Unfortunately, this is much easier said than done. Few of us were taught to think about what we like sexually, let alone be able to bravely and openly ask for those things. Fear of rejection or judgment often results in silencing your intimacy needs, especially when it comes to sex. This activity will help you both think about your sexual desires and begin a conversation about getting those needs met.

> **SUPPLIES**
>
> Two separate notebooks or scrap paper
>
> Two writing utensils

INSTRUCTIONS

1. Each partner uses their separate notebook to write down three columns. Title them "Yes," "Maybe," and "No."

2. Write down the sexual or sensual activities that are your must-haves ("Yes"), that you're interested in exploring ("Maybe"), and your hard passes ("No").

3. If you get stuck thinking of needs and desires, feel free to use the ideas table on page 43 to help inspire you.

4. Before you share your menu with your partner, remember this is a vulnerable activity. Be mindful not to communicate judgment or disdain for what your partner has written, even if you're not on board with it.

5. Share your menus with each other by either reading them aloud or swapping your notebooks. Ask your partner any questions you have about their preferences. Take extra care to never lie to each other on your "Nos."

IDEAS FOR YESES/MAYBES/NOS

- Making out
- Sensual massages
- Power dynamics
- Role play
- Dirty talk
- Oral sex (giving)
- Oral sex (receiving)
- Using a vibrator together
- Being blindfolded
- Debriefing after a new sexual experience

IDEAS FOR NOS

- Not checking if I've had an orgasm
- Pressuring me to have sex
- Lack of aftercare
- Lack of foreplay
- Talking or not talking during sex
- Not asking for consent before sexual touching
- Focusing only on penetration

LET'S TALK ABOUT IT

Was it easier for you to create your menu or tell your partner about your needs? Where are the areas that you overlap? Congratulate yourselves for taking a major step toward building your sexual intimacy. This endeavor is rarely easy or comfortable but will result in more satisfying and fulfilling sexual experiences.

WATER BALLOON FIGHT

Estimated time: **30 MINUTES**

It's no wonder why so many reality TV dating shows feature dates where the contestants are forced out of their comfort zone into adventurous or thrill-seeking situations. We feel closer to our partner when we have gone through something scary, thrilling, or brand-new together. Fear, excitement, and uncertainty can bring us closer because they require us to be vulnerable and put our trust in each other. Scientifically speaking, when we take risks together or try new experiences, our brains release dopamine, the same chemical that gets released in the beginning stage of our relationship. When you do a thrilling activity together, the chemical reaction you experienced when you first met gets replicated, bringing you back to a time often described as containing a spark of excitement and newness.

> **SUPPLIES**
>
> Water
>
> Two dozen medium water balloons
>
> One large bucket
>
> Two dry towels

INSTRUCTIONS

1. Pick a location for your water balloon fight at a local park or your backyard.

2. Fill the water balloons with water. Put them in a bucket for easy carrying.

3. Head to your location with your balloons. Remember to practice this step with compassion.

4. Agree on any rules, such as no hitting in the eyes or to stop when someone says "stop."

5. Place the bucket between you. Walk back twenty paces.

6. Count down together from ten. Once you get to zero, run as fast as you can to the bucket and start throwing water balloons at each other.

7. Once the balloons are gone, dry off with your towels. (Together, dispose of the used balloons.)

LET'S TALK ABOUT IT

What were the feelings you had before, during, and after the water balloon fight? Perhaps you felt nervous anticipation before and fear and excitement during. Doing something outside the box that gets our heart rate up with our partner can be a fun way to experience excitement and newness again.

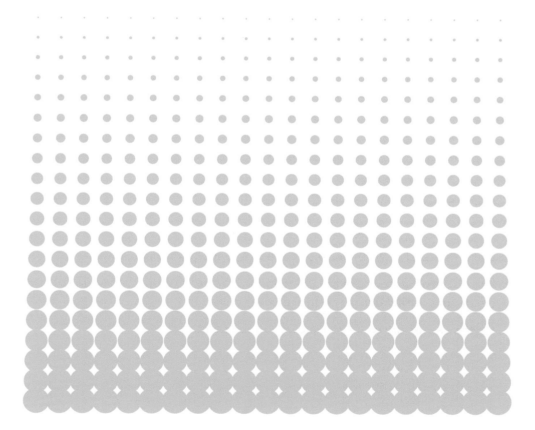

MAKE LOVE THROUGH ART

Estimated time: **20 MINUTES**

The more you build intimacy between yourselves, the more difficult it can be to take new and exciting sensual risks with each other. Sometimes this is because the safer you feel with your partner, the less risk there inherently is, which can result in less of what makes a sexual experience exciting and erotic. Other times, it's because partners can get stuck in the same pattern of romance. This isn't completely a bad thing. When you both learn what the other needs to feel sexy or have a good intimate experience, there may be less of an emphasis on exploring new sexy areas, as you may already know the exact things that turn each other on. Whether you know each other well or have only recently started dating, this activity will give you both a new and exciting way to physically connect with each other. After you're done, you'll have a homemade piece of modern art that both of you can look at and remember a fun and sexy time you shared!

> ### SUPPLIES
>
> **4 oz bottle of washable nontoxic paint**
>
> **10 x 12-inch plastic tarp or painter's drop cloth**
>
> **3.5 x 4.5-inch treated white canvas**

INSTRUCTIONS

1. Roll the tarp or drop cloth out on a surface you both can lie down on comfortably.

2. Place the canvas on top of the tarp.

3. Pour the paint on the canvas.

4. Get undressed or wear clothes you're okay with getting paint on.

5. Use your bodies to move the paint around the canvas together while you create an abstract design on top of your canvas.

6. Let the canvas dry while you shower off the paint.

LET'S TALK ABOUT IT

What did you enjoy about this activity? What about this activity felt new, exciting, or risky? Engaging in new sexy or sensual experiences with each other is a great way to keep things fresh between you two, which will help keep your spark alive!

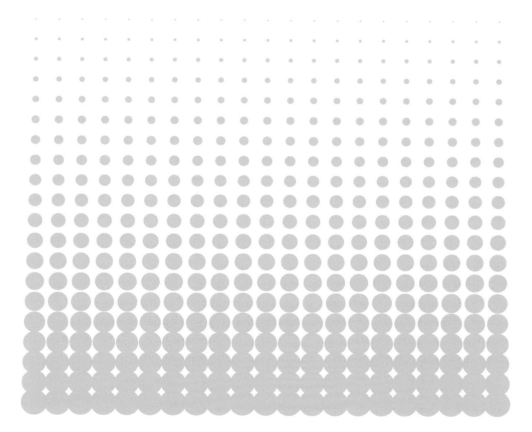

CHAPTER SIX

UNDERSTANDING FEELINGS OF JEALOUSY

ALTHOUGH JEALOUSY IS a feeling many can relate to, the experience of it rarely feels comfortable in the moment. Jealousy can bring on intense emotions such as sadness, anger, insecurity, fear, or resentment. It can include any thoughts and feelings related to a real or perceived threat to your relationship or an experience of having an inequitable number of resources. Although the presence of jealousy may suggest an issue in your relationship, it's natural to feel jealous at times. If you struggle with depression, anxiety, low self-esteem, or trauma, you may be even more likely to experience jealousy at times due to old wounds resurfacing or a belief that your worth is tied to the love you receive from your partner. Although jealousy is natural and common, it has the potential to impact how you behave in your relationship. Jealousy can bring you closer together, push you further apart, or do a combination of both, depending on how partners handle the situation. This chapter will help you better understand your feelings of jealousy, create space for those feelings by regulating and managing them, and help you effectively communicate with your partner.

CREATING SPACE FOR JEALOUSY

Estimated time: **5 MINUTES**

Feelings of jealousy are difficult to sit with, but it's import-ant to remember that your feelings are different from your actions. Separating feelings from actions can feel impossi-ble, as the time between your feeling and your subsequent behavior can go by in the blink of an eye. This activity can help couples slow down their emotional processing so they can think more clearly about the best path forward.

SUPPLIES

INSTRUCTIONS

1. Sit upright and close your eyes.

2. Take three slow, deep breaths. Notice your breath flowing in and out.

3. Mentally scan your body from head to toe. Observe the different sensations in your body.

4. Zoom into the areas where you are feeling jealousy. Observe the feeling closely, without judgment. Let your thoughts come and go. Stay focused on the feeling. Where does it start and end in your body?

5. As you observe, breathe. Imagine your breath flowing in and around this feeling.

6. Allow the feeling to expand in your body, giving it as much space as it needs.

7. See how long you can allow the emotion to exist, even if it feels uncomfortable.

8. When you're ready, open your eyes.

LET'S TALK ABOUT IT
By observing feelings without judgment, you can reclaim the power feelings have over your actions. Practice this the next time you feel a big and intense emotion and see how it impacts your mood and behavior.

WORRY JAR

Estimated time: **15 MINUTES**

When your worst fears take up space in your mind without any release or reprieve, they take on more power over time and begin to feel increasingly real. When fears feel like they will imminently come to fruition, you'll begin to act in ways that can be destructive to your relationship because the fear suggests you should act with unnecessary urgency. This activity will reduce the power your fears have over you and help you honor your fears by acknowledging and releasing them. You'll also discover if your fears are unfounded or ridiculous and determine if a supportive conversation with your partner is needed.

SUPPLIES

Several pieces of scrap paper

Writing utencils

Jar

INSTRUCTIONS

1. Think of something that makes you feel jealous in your relationship. Think about what you're most afraid of regarding this situation. Write it down on one piece of scrap paper. Fold it up and put it in your worry jar.

2. Now answer the question "What would that possibly result in?" Write that answer down on your next scrap of paper, fold it up, and put it in the worry jar.

3. Assume that result happens. Now answer the question "And then what?" Write that result down on your next scrap of paper, fold it up, and put it in the worry jar.

4. Think about the fears you wrote down. Ask yourself: Are these fears founded? Are they real? Is there anything you might communicate to your partner about your fears?

5. If you answered yes to the final question, plan a time to share your fear with your partner by reading your scrap papers aloud to them.

LET'S TALK ABOUT IT

What did you notice about your fears the deeper you dug? How did writing your fears down impact how you felt about them? Did it make you more willing to talk to your partner about them? Keep this worry jar nearby to use in the future. Add more fears to it and throw away old fears you no longer have. Take out the jar every so often to read through your fears, allow them to exist, and decide what next step to take.

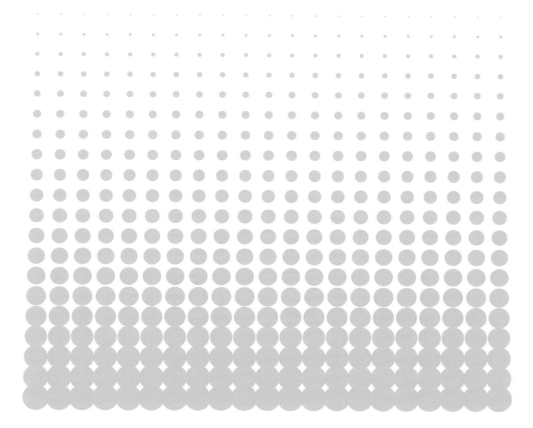

LEARNING FROM JEALOUSY

Estimated time: **20 MINUTES**

The activities in this chapter have been individually focused until now. That's because *you* are the main person responsible for your own feelings, including jealousy. No one can do anything to change or impact your emotions, except you. To build a secure and strong foundation in our relationship, it's important to take care of our own emotions by intentionally feeling them before we act on them. By taking the time to fully *feel* our emotions, we can more thoughtfully think through what we need in our relationship or from our partner moving forward.

> **SUPPLIES**
>
> none

INSTRUCTIONS

1. One person communicates one experience that triggers jealousy in your relationship. Use the phrase "I feel jealous when _____." Be careful not to criticize your partner or use extreme words like "always" and "never." (Example: "I feel jealous when you got a raise because it reminded me of how little I make.")

2. The other person listens without judgment or defensiveness. Hear what is being asked without asking for an explanation.

3. The first person uses the needs bank on page 53 to determine a need that would support you with your jealousy. It may be an emotional need like an increased sensitivity from your partner when they discuss money or a concrete need like brainstorming how to make more money.

4. The second person thanks the first for sharing something vulnerable.

5. The second person communicates whether that need can be met. Ask questions if you need clarification. Speak up if there's something that would help you satisfy this need for them. (For example, reassurance; pointing out when you've done it right.)

6. Switch positions and begin the activity again.

NEEDS BANK

❏ I need you to initiate sex.

❏ I need to know when you find me attractive.

❏ I need you to ask about my day.

❏ I need you to greet me when I come home.

❏ I need you to take initiative on chores.

❏ I need you to make eye contact with me.

❏ I need us to spend time away together.

❏ I need you to plan a date.

❏ I need to see my friends more often alone.

❏ I need you to be mindful of my sensitivity.

LET'S TALK ABOUT IT

What was it like to see your jealousy as an unmet need? Was it difficult to identify a need? When you take a closer look at jealousy, you begin to see this emotion as an opportunity to become closer with your partner while you get your needs met.

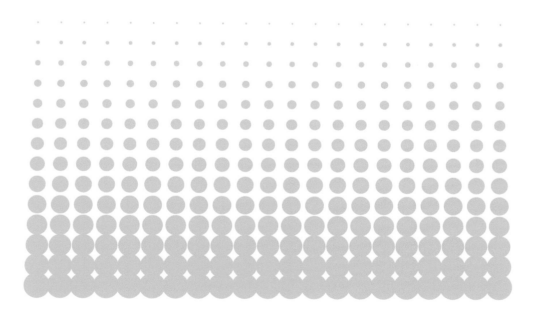

SPOTTING UNHEALTHY JEALOUSY

Estimated time: **20 MINUTES**

SUPPLIES

While it's important to sit with jealous feelings and communicate them to each other once you have fully felt those feelings, it's equally important to discern between behaviors stemming from jealousy that are healthy and those that are problematic or abusive. Jealousy is a normal and common emotion. However, when you act out on your jealousy in possessive or controlling ways, you're creating or perpetuating an unhealthy dynamic in your relationship. Understanding the signs of abusive or problematic behaviors both in yourself and in your partner is imperative to making sure that you're experiencing and cultivating a relationship built on mutual respect.

INSTRUCTIONS

1. Play the game Never Have I Ever, except make each experience you share about a romantic experience related to jealousy.

2. Each put up ten fingers. One at a time, each partner share something they have never experienced in a romantic relationship related to jealousy by saying: "Never have I ever . . ." These experiences can be something you have never done or something a partner has never done. (Examples: "Never have I ever checked a partner's texts without their consent," "Never have I ever asked to check a partner's text messages.") If you get stuck, draw from the nevers bank on page 55.

3. When one partner shares an experience, if the other partner has personally experienced that, put one finger down.

4. The partner left with the most fingers by the end of ten rounds wins.

NEVERS BANK

- ❏ Insisted a partner spend all their time together with me
- ❏ Experienced extreme suspicion or paranoia
- ❏ Demanded unreasonably frequent check-ins when apart
- ❏ Pressured a partner to be intimate
- ❏ Felt bad when my partner experienced success

- ❏ Controlled what a partner wears
- ❏ Controlled who a partner hangs out with
- ❏ Monitored communications with others
- ❏ Spoke put-downs or name-calling
- ❏ Threatened a partner
- ❏ Embarrassed a partner in public

LET'S TALK ABOUT IT

Were any behaviors shared that either of you found unacceptable? What behaviors have more of a gray area? Acting out of jealousy doesn't automatically mean you're abusive or problematic. It's important to remember that abuse is a pattern of power and controlling behaviors that build over time. To disrupt this pattern and build a healthy relationship, each partner must take accountability for their jealous feelings, recognize when you act in problematic ways from those emotions, and communicate your needs effectively instead of trying to control your partner.

SEPARATING FEELINGS FROM FACTS

Estimated time: **10 MINUTES**

Jealousy can often snowball into a fear that worst-case scenarios will happen. This thinking pattern is called "catastrophizing." Catastrophizing means becoming consumed by obsessive, emotional thoughts that can end up being detrimental to a relationship. This activity will help slow down your thoughts and feelings by acknowledging that they are thoughts and feelings, *not* facts.

SUPPLIES

INSTRUCTIONS

1. Sit or stand across from each other. Choose an experience that caused you, as a couple, to experience fear, anger, jealousy, or sadness. Close your eyes and take yourselves back to the moment. How did you feel?

2. Next, each person does an internal check-in. Notice the thoughts that accompany your emotions. Each partner tries to summarize their thoughts into one sentence. For example, "I will end up alone."

3. Each partner verbalizes their thought by speaking the sentence aloud. Repeat it once more for each other.

4. Take turns adding the phrase "I'm having the thought" in front of the previous statements. (Example: "I'm having the thought that I will end up alone.") Say that sentence aloud. Repeat it once more.

5. Add the phrase "I notice" in front of the previous statement. Say that sentence aloud. Repeat it once more.

LET'S TALK ABOUT IT

How did it feel to put more space between your thoughts and yourself? This process, called defusion, gives thoughts less credibility by acknowledging that they are not unequivocal truths but are instead thoughts that can be used to separate from the self. Defusion can help us better manage our emotions and act with intentionality instead of our jealousy-driven thoughts.

CHAPTER SEVEN

RESOLVING CONFLICT

CONFLICTS ARE DESTINED to occur in all relationships, especially your romantic ones. Fighting with your partner is not necessarily an indicator of issues in your relationship. But the *way* you fight can have major impacts on how you feel and experience your romantic partnership. If you walk away from a conflict feeling respected, heard, and understood, conflicts are productive, useful, and necessary. However, if you tend to walk away from disagreements feeling shamed, blamed, and misunderstood, fights will most likely keep occurring with little chance of resolution and a high probability of emotional turmoil. When conflicts continuously don't end well, it's common for one or both of you to feel it's better to stay quiet than get into another argument. Learning how to fight effectively as well as repair and reconnect following a disagreement is imperative for the overall health of your relationship. This chapter will help you learn how to fight fairly using open and honest communication and how to build your confidence. Then, whenever you disagree, you'll have the tools to come together to talk productively and find creative solutions that leave you both feeling respected and understood.

BE SPECIFIC

Estimated time: **15 MINUTES**

One of the easiest ways to get into the same fight repeatedly is by being too general about your feelings and needs. Imagine a mother telling her child: "Why can't you just *behave*?" That child will most likely walk away with a different understanding of what "behaving" means than the mother intended, because her request was too general. When you get into altercations with each other, it's important to practice specificity so that you walk away with a mutual understanding.

> **SUPPLIES**
>
> Piece of artwork (online)
>
> Art supplies of choice

INSTRUCTIONS

1. Search online for a piece of artwork. (Do not share the image with your partner.)

2. Your partner acts as the artist while you will act as the director.

3. Use verbal directions to communicate what your partner needs to draw (or paint, paste, etc.) in order to replicate the artwork. Be as specific as possible in your instructions.

4. At any point, ask clarifying questions if your partner isn't being specific enough.

5. Once you have communicated every component of the artwork, check together to see how well your communication resulted in replicating the artwork.

 **LET'S TALK ABOUT IT**
What was difficult about being as specific as possible? What was difficult about trying to rely completely on someone else's directions? The more specific you can get for your partner and the more you feel comfortable clarifying what you don't understand, the easier it will be to overcome misunderstandings and get on the same page during a conflict.

KEEPING IT BRIEF

Estimated time: **10 MINUTES**

Fights go south quickly when we use too many words to communicate. Remember in Charlie Brown when the teacher drones on and it sounds like "Womp, womp, womp, womp"? Communicating in large paragraphs without pausing to check for understanding will often lead the person listening to tune out or misunderstand the overall message. This results in miscommunications, shutdowns, and escalations, especially since the longer you talk, the more opportunities there are for your partner to take issue with your sentiments. This activity will help you practice brevity so you can get your point across succinctly to promote understanding.

INSTRUCTIONS

1. Facing each other, one person tells the other about a recent upsetting event using only ten words at a time. Every time you hit two words, take a pause.

2. The second person communicates what you heard. Begin with "What I hear you saying is . . ." and then repeat back what you heard, in your own words. You do not have a ten-word restriction, but be mindful that your responses aren't overly wordy.

3. Respond to your partner, continuing to explain your point of view using only ten words at a time until you have fully communicated your experience.

4. Switch positions and repeat.

LET'S TALK ABOUT IT
How difficult was it for you to keep your message under ten words at a time? What was the experience of being the listener like? Being brief becomes even more difficult when we are upset with each other, so this is good practice to prepare for those times.

LET'S COMPROMISE

Estimated time: **20 MINUTES**

Compromising with each other is key to overcoming conflicts in your relationship. When one person always wins, relationships feel off balance and unfair, which builds resentment. Compromising on both sides helps build trust that what is most important isn't winning but instead making sure that you both feel heard and understood. In order to compromise, remember that you're working to get on the same page with someone you care about, instead of trying to be the "right" one. This activity will help both of you operate less often from a winner/loser mindset and more from discovering areas of flexibility around a gridlocked topic.

SUPPLIES

One playing die

One piece of scrap paper

Writing utensil

INSTRUCTIONS

1. Pick a topic that you both fight over often. (Common examples include cleaning your shared space, co-parenting, spending time with other family members, going out versus staying in, initiating sex, etc.)

2. The first person speaks the issue out loud, in a short sentence that describes both of your perspectives. (For example: You like to stay in most weekends while the other likes to go out.)

3. Next, that person rolls a die.

4. Whatever number appears on the die, think of that number of ways your partner can be flexible around the issue. (For example: If you roll a two, think of two potential solutions, like just going out with friends, going out only one night of the week, etc.)

5. Taking turns, the other person rolls the die and repeats steps one through three.

6. Write down all your favorite solutions.

7. Choose one or two of your favorite solutions to try this week.

LET'S TALK ABOUT IT
What new information did you both learn about this topic? How difficult was it to come up with your areas of flexibility? The important part of this exercise is not the solution you choose but rather being able to respond to a conflict with a spirit of flexibility so that you can both feel like you're willing to make some adjustments to solve the issue together.

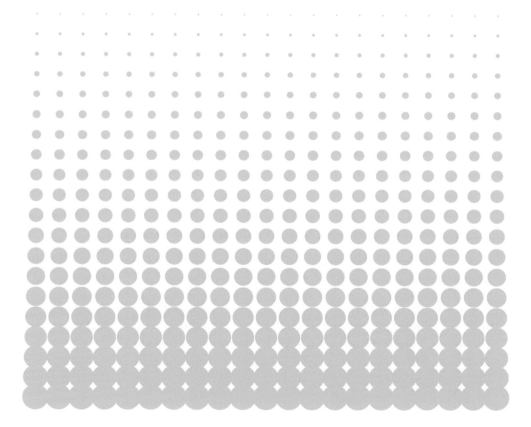

TRACKING HEARTBEATS TOGETHER

Estimated time: **20 MINUTES**

When partners fight, one or both people can experience intense emotions, causing you to say things you don't mean. Or you may completely forget what was said because you were "seeing red." Sound familiar? This experience of being "emotionally flooded" raises our heart rates and makes it difficult to form logical thoughts and communicate effectively. In times like these, it's good to take a break to reset and calm down. This activity will help both of you take a time-out by noticing when your heart rate goes up. You'll also practice agreeing on a time to come back together once you both feel calm.

> ### SUPPLIES
>
> Two heart rate monitors (a simple oximeter or using fingers to take your pulse)
>
> ———
>
> Timer

INSTRUCTIONS

1. Set the timer for ten minutes.

2. Each partner puts on an oximeter and measures your resting heart rate.

3. Start doing ten jumping jacks followed by ten burpees. Repeat this set when you've finished.

4. As you exercise, keep a close eye on your oximeter.

5. As soon as either of your heart rates goes over one hundred bpm, stop exercising and call for a time-out by saying "I need a time-out." The other partner must respect and accept the time-out, pausing the timer.

6. Take five minutes to separate and get your heart rate back down.

7. During your time-out, each does a solo activity that normally makes you feel calm and relaxed—listen to music, draw, or stretch, etc.

8. At the end of the time-out, begin your jumping jacks and burpees again until ten minutes have elapsed on the timer. If either person's heart rate goes above one hundred bpm, take another time-out for five minutes.

LET'S TALK ABOUT IT

How hard was it to take space in the middle of your exercise? Was it easier to take space as the person who had the higher heart rate or as the partner being told to take a break? What did you notice about your body when you were transitioning to a time-out? This activity is not about solving the issue but learning to stop conversations before they become harmful.

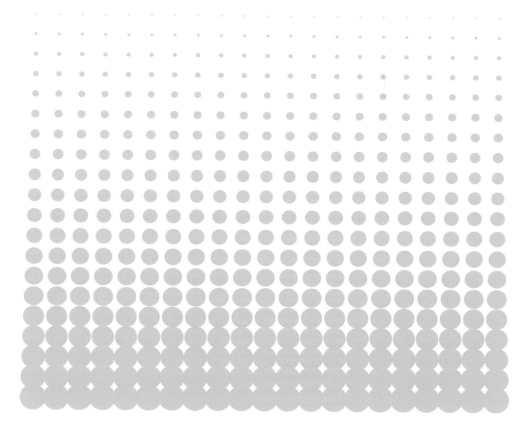

IN YOUR PARTNER'S SHOES

Estimated time: **20 MINUTES**

When you get into gridlocked arguments with your partner, it's usually because you're having difficulty stepping out of your perspective and into theirs. The more you stay firmly planted in your point of view without acknowledging the reality and legitimacy of your loved one's viewpoint, the more likely it is that your partner will also stay firmly planted in their belief system. Research shows that the existence of mutual and reciprocal influence in a relationship promotes feelings of satisfaction and happiness. But *how* you communicate your perspective may make it difficult for your partner to hear you, especially if you're blaming or berating. This activity mirrors the process of tracking your physiological experience while engaging with your partner so that you could both practice how to respond accordingly by taking space to cool down before coming back together.

> **SUPPLIES**
>
> Two chairs
>
> One stopwatch or timer

INSTRUCTIONS

1. Sit down on two chairs facing each other.

2. Decide on a conversation topic that you've discussed before several times but have yet to reach a consensus on. Instead of discussing it as you have in the past, this time you're going to switch roles. One person will act as and speak with the talking style and mannerisms of the second person and vice versa.

3. Set the timer for five minutes and discuss the topic. To the best of your ability, pretend to be your partner by communicating from their perspective in the way they would communicate it.

4. After five minutes, switch roles, switch seats, and communicate as yourself with your own perspective, adjusting any behavior that was reflected to you by your partner that you want to shift.

5. When the time is up, give each other a hug and say one thing to validate your partner's perspective. Start with the phrase "I can understand how you feel that way because . . ."

LET'S TALK ABOUT IT

Watching your partner behave as you gave you the unique experience of seeing how you come off to your loved one. By acting as your partner, you showcased your understanding of your partner's position and had an opportunity to give them feedback on how they come off. Validating the legitimacy of each other's perspectives, even if you don't completely agree, helps build trust that you are a team that is flexible and adaptable based on each other's needs and viewpoints.

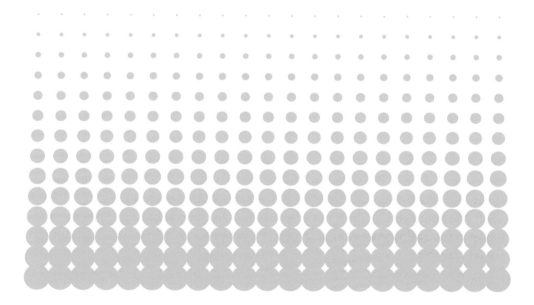

CHAPTER EIGHT

PET PEEVES

ALL COUPLES HAVE things that bother them about each other, also known as pet peeves. Ironically, it can be the attributes that first drew you to each other that may become frustrating or off-putting as time goes on. Pet peeves are separate from the bigger fundamental conflicts or disagreements that come from having different core values. Instead, pet peeves are those smaller annoyances that may not be deal breakers but still come with their own set of frustrations. When pet peeves pile up or aren't dealt with over time, there can be major consequences in a romantic relationship, such as more frequent arguing or feeling attacked, misunderstood, or underappreciated by each other. It's important for couples to know both your own pet peeves and your partner's pet peeves. Neither of you may be able to totally change the main areas that make up your partner's personality (nor should your relationship require this!). But you should be aware of the things that bother you about your partner, not only to minimize conflicts but also to try to behave in the opposite ways of each other's pet peeves, which will positively impact your relationship.

PET PEEVE HUMAN KNOT

Estimated time: **20 MINUTES**

Generally discussing your pet peeves in a non-accusatory way can help partners gain that information without feeling attacked or as though they must fix something immediately. This activity will help you start a conversation around sharing pet peeves so that you can be aware of each other's preferences without feeling criticized.

SUPPLIES

Colored construction paper

Scissors

Plastic tarp or bedsheet

Tape

INSTRUCTIONS

1. Cut out red, blue, green, and yellow circles and tape them in rows on a medium-size tarp or bedsheet.

2. Together, stand at one side of the sheet.

3. Take turns calling out a color for your partner to place a hand or foot on.

4. When you land on red, share one pet peeve that you experience while at work or school.

5. When you land on yellow, share one pet peeve that you experience while doing a favorite activity or hobby.

6. When you land on green, share one pet peeve you experience while on a date.

7. When you land on blue, share one pet peeve you experienced in childhood.

8. End the game when one partner falls on the ground.

LET'S TALK ABOUT IT
What surprised you about each other's pet peeves? Did you have anything in common? Sharing your general pet peeves helps to give each other a sense of your likes and dislikes, which will set you both up for greater success in your day-to-day interactions.

ACT OUT YOUR PET PEEVES

Estimated time: **20 MINUTES**

Pointing out your annoyances about each other can go very wrong very quickly when you're not careful to phrase your critique in a specific and intentional way. It's important to frame your message as a complaint and not a character assassination, meaning it's better to complain about a frustrating *situation* and not criticize who your partner fundamentally *is* as a person. For example, saying "I hate it when you are late" has a better chance of being met with less defensiveness than if you were to say, "I hate how inconsiderate you are." This activity will help you practice how to complain about a situation—not criticize your partner's character—by acting out your pet peeves in front of each other.

> **SUPPLIES**
>
> Scraps of paper
>
> Two writing utensils
>
> Timer
>
> Hat

INSTRUCTIONS

1. Play a game of charades, but instead of acting out popular media, famous people, and places, you'll act out your pet-peeve situations.

2. You each write down five pet peeves on scraps of paper. Phrase your pet peeves as situations, not personalities, using the example above as a reference.

3. Fold and place the papers in a hat.

4. Set the timer for one minute. One person picks a piece of scrap paper and acts out the peeve for the second person to guess before time runs out. Remember you cannot talk, only act out the pet peeve you picked.

5. The round is over when your partner guesses correctly or when time runs out. If someone acts out the other's pet peeves, explain your pet peeve with more detail.

6. Next, the second person selects another scrap of paper. Repeat steps 4 and 5, switching positions.

7. Once you act out each pet peeve, the game ends.

LET'S TALK ABOUT IT
What was difficult about acting out an annoying situation instead of a personality trait? What did you learn about each other's preferences from their pet peeves? When you both describe what each other does that annoys you instead of making a comment on your partner's personality, you will both have a much better chance of getting your needs met when pet peeves show up in your relationship.

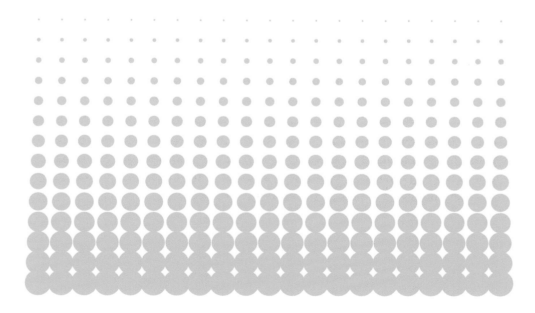

STARS FOR GOOD BEHAVIOR

Estimated time: **15 MINUTES**

Constantly pointing out each other's wrongdoing in your relationship can feel very disheartening for both partners. The complaining partner feels like they are rarely getting their needs met, while the partner who is the subject of the complaints feels like they can't do anything right. Building regular instances of noticing good behavior in each other is much more motivating than only being told when you have done something wrong. Acknowledging when your partner behaves as you like will create a positive climate within your relationship that both partners will benefit from.

SUPPLIES

Two pieces of paper

Art supplies

Stickers (optional)

INSTRUCTIONS

1. Each partner picks a specific pet peeve that you have about your partner. (Examples: leaving the toilet seat up, lateness, interrupting, etc.)

2. Each draw and decorate a chart that includes ten open spaces for your partner. (You'll find an example on page 71.) Make sure the behaviors are as specific as possible and phrased in the positive. (Example: putting the toilet seat down, arriving on time, letting you finish speaking before they chime in.)

3. Each partner chooses the reward that they would most like after they have demonstrated the positive behavior ten times. (Examples: a fifteen-minute massage, choosing the movie or restaurant during your next date night, etc.)

4. Put your behavior charts somewhere that you both can see them to track your progress over the next week. Each time your partner does the behavior you're looking for, mark the slot with a star or a sticker. Once your partner has done the behavior ten times, give them their reward.

LET'S TALK ABOUT IT

How hard was it to choose a specific pet peeve? What do you think will be difficult about noticing when your partner does the positive version of your pet peeve? How does it feel when your partner notices your good behavior? When you ask your partner to do something differently for you, it will always be more motivating to tell them what they *can* do instead of what they shouldn't do.

Examples	Good Behavior	Reward
Partner 1	Punctuality	Choose date night
Partner 2	Waiting to speak	15-minute massage

EMPATHY OR PROBLEM-SOLVING?

Estimated time: **20 MINUTES**

When we're frustrated by something in our everyday life, we often want one of two things from our partner: empathy or problem solving. Empathy is when our partner steps into our emotional world by validating and acknowledging our experience. Problem-solving is when our partner joins in on brainstorming and offers concrete solutions for our issue. Knowing whether we want empathy or problem-solving can help us prevent a lot of frustration that arises when our partner has done something that's bothered or upset us. Having a partner who can meet us where we are when we're upset and give us what we need will deepen our intimacy.

SUPPLIES

Two separate notebooks

Writing utensils

INSTRUCTIONS

1. Read the scenarios on page 73 out loud and write them in your separate notebooks.

2. Note for each whether you would prefer empathy or problem-solving from your partner in these scenarios.

3. Whenever you select "empathy," complete the "say" statement with words your partner could say that would feel best to hear in the moment. (Examples: "I'm so sorry." "I cannot imagine." Or simply "I am here.")

4. Discuss with your partner whether you chose empathy or problem-solving for each situation. If you have a reason why you chose what you did, feel free to share it.

5. Finally, both partners share what empathic statements felt best for you to hear for the situations where you prefer empathy.

6. Ask any follow-up questions you have for each other.

SCENARIOS

Forgetting something you previously talked about: empathy//problem-solving

Say: _____

Doing a household chore "incorrectly": empathy//problem-solving

Say: _____

Interrupting you: empathy//problem-solving

Say: _____

Not prioritizing a date night: empathy//problem-solving

Say: _____

Being on their phone too often: empathy//problem-solving

Say: _____

Loud eating/drinking: empathy//problem-solving

Say: _____

Chronic lateness: empathy//problem-solving

Say: _____

LET'S TALK ABOUT IT

Did you notice that you prefer problem-solving or empathy more? What do you notice about the type of empathic responses that you desire? Knowing what you need when you're frustrated will give your partner a leg up in giving you the emotional care and safety that helps to manage conflicts.

CHARACTER COCKTAILS

Estimated time: **15 MINUTES**

Frequently pointing out the aspects of your partner's character or behavior that you don't like can negatively impact their self-esteem, even though this may be completely unintentional. Building an environment of appreciation for each other is important in your relationship so that you can both feel that you partner basically *likes* you as a person. Trying to strive for a balance of four compliments to one criticism at any given time is a great way to ensure that neither of you is being overly critical nor damaging each other's confidence.

INSTRUCTIONS

1. Each partner creates a cocktail (or mocktail) using five ingredients that represent your partner.

2. Four ingredients should represent your partner's strengths and one should symbolize a pet peeve you have of your partner. (Examples: simple syrup for sweetness, jalapeño for your partner's sassy retorts, etc.)

3. As you each make your partner's cocktail, explain why you chose each ingredient.

4. When you have both finished mixing your drink, swap cocktails and drink each other's creation made especially for you!

LET'S TALK ABOUT IT

How was it coming up with ingredients that represent your partner? Was it easier to find ingredients for your partner's strengths or for the one pet peeve? Remembering to balance each negative comment with extra compliments is an important way to build and maintain an appreciative environment for each other, which will make it easier for both of you to hear those inevitable criticism without feeling hurt.

CHAPTER NINE

ACCEPTING AND GRANTING FORGIVENESS

ACCEPTING AND GRANTING forgiveness are two necessary practices in creating and maintaining a strong and healthy relationship. Forgiving yourself and your partner for wrongdoing frees both partners from building up bitterness, contempt, or resentment over time. When you struggle to forgive yourself for your mistakes, shame and guilt can make you shut down or seek comfort outside your relationship, which, in turn, creates distance between you two. When you struggle to forgive your partner, it can be very difficult to overcome smaller daily conflicts because you are holding on to past unresolved pain. It's important to work through letting go of the past to create a better future together. But forgiveness does not mean that either of you needs to accept or condone mistreatment or abuse from the other. Not all behaviors deserve forgiveness; what someone chooses to forgive varies from person to person. Forgiveness requires a willingness to look past your partner's transgression to move on and hopefully grow from the experience, making your relationship stronger. The activities in this chapter will help you take accountability for your missteps, heal from resentment, and move toward creating a deeper bond.

A MUSICAL APOLOGY

Estimated time: **20 TO 30 MINUTES**

SUPPLIES

Both partner's personal music collection

Forgiving yourself and being forgiven by your partner is only possible when you take accountability. When you make a mistake, you may experience feelings of shame, guilt, or fear that are tough to sit with, which may lead you to dismiss your behavior by making it seem not as bad. When you do this, you rob your relationship of the opportunity to deal with what actually happened so that you can both fully move on. One of the hardest parts of taking accountability is putting it into words. This activity will help you do this.

INSTRUCTIONS

1. Each partner goes through their own music library and picks out five songs that have lyrics describing what went wrong during the last argument they had with their partner. These songs can be about the things you did wrong or can describe what you were feeling that made you make those mistakes.

2. Once you have each picked your five songs, create separate playlists for your chosen songs.

3. Give your playlist a title that summarizes your accountability (Example: "Shutting Down," or "I Need to Be Right.")

4. Share your playlists with each other, explaining why you chose the songs you did.

5. Listen to both playlists together while cuddling.

LET'S TALK ABOUT IT
What feelings came up for you as you looked for songs? What feelings did you have listening to your partner's playlist? Taking accountability and seeing your partner take accountability are necessary steps in repairing and healing after an argument.

LAUGHING YOGA FOR FORGIVENESS

Estimated time: **10 MINUTES**

Bringing intentional humor into conflicts can reduce stress and tension. Humor lets partners know that not all conflicts are deal breakers, signaling that sharing frustrations doesn't have to result in a total breakdown. This activity will help you relieve stress through laughter which you can call upon the next time you're in a tense moment together.

SUPPLIES

INSTRUCTIONS

1. Both partners stand facing each other and begin clapping your own hands together, keeping hands flat and fingers lining up perfectly to stimulate your pressure points.

2. Clap with a 1, 2, 1-2-3 rhythm for five rounds.

3. In unison, start chanting "ho, ha-ha-ha" as you clap along to that beat. Repeat five times.

4. Swing your arms slowly above your heads in a V shape, stretching your arms toward the ceiling and planting your feet firmly on the ground. With your arms toward the ceiling, hold your breath in for five seconds and gently lean back, looking at the ceiling.

5. Release your breath slowly as you bring your hands to your sides and come back to center in unison. Repeat three times.

6. Repeat steps 4 and 5, but this time, when you release your breath and arms, give a big laugh from your belly. Repeat five times.

7. To end, make eye contact with your partner and give each other a big hug, a high five, and one last big laugh from your diaphragm.

LET'S TALK ABOUT IT
Sharing some humor with each other during or after a conflict, if both parties are open to it, can be a great way to bring some lightness into your relationship as it relieves you both of putting the pressure of taking all discussions too seriously.

FORGIVENESS TREASURE MAP

Estimated time: **20 MINUTES**

When either of you has upset the other, the partner who got hurt may find it difficult to move on. The partner who did the hurting may not know what's needed to move on. This can result in conflicts dragging out for days or weeks unnecessarily. When you're hurt, sometimes you may want to make your partner pay for their behavior. Be careful with this! It will never result in you both moving on in the spirit of growth and has the risk of making your partner fearful of ever upsetting you again. A healthier way to move on once you've forgiven your partner is to give them a map to help them get back into your good graces. That way, you get what you need to move on, and your partner has an idea of how to do better in their treatment of you for the future. This collaging activity will help both of you think about what your needs are following a situation where one of you hurt the other.

SUPPLIES

Scissors

Old magazines

Glue or tape

Two pieces of card stock or construction paper

INSTRUCTIONS

1. Browse through old magazines, looking for words or pictures that represent what you need after having your feelings hurt or being mistreated. Maybe you need space, snuggles, specific actions, words of reassurance, or a combination of all four.

2. Cut out any pictures or phrases that represent your needs following hurt feelings and paste them on your own piece of paper, making a collage.

3. When you both are finished with your collages, share your artwork with each other, explaining why you chose the pictures or phrases that you did.

4. Ask each other questions to better understand your partner's needs. (Think: frequency, intensity, and duration. Example: How much space do you need? How much time should we devote to debriefing about what happened?)

LET'S TALK ABOUT IT
Where are your similarities in what you need after your partner has done something wrong? Do either of you tend to need more space or greater closeness following a fight? What did you learn about your partner? Giving your partner a map to get back into your good graces is not only a great way to move on from a fight but is also a great way to restate your needs and boundaries going forward in your relationship.

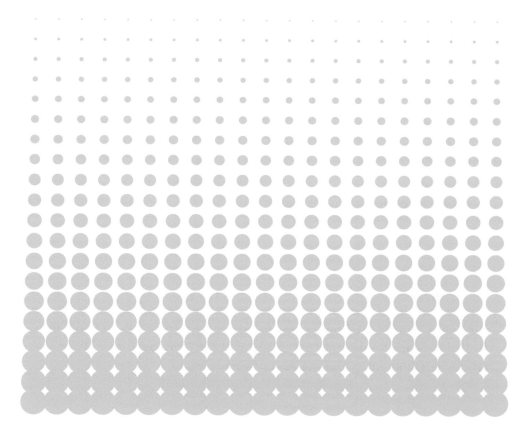

NEW YEAR, NEW US

Estimated time: **20 MINUTES**

Many cultures have a New Year's tradition that consist of processing and making peace with the past in order to move forward into the future. In your romantic relationship, you both may be holding on to negative feelings, hurtful words, and painful experiences that occurred between you during the past year. When you hold on too tightly to these experiences, resentment builds and harms your relationship, making it difficult to move on and start fresh. Nelson Mandela once said, "Resentment is like drinking poison and then hoping it will kill your enemies." This activity will help you both think about what experiences and feelings you need to release and keep in the past so that you can start working on your future together.

> **SUPPLIES**
>
> Clay (you can find simple homemade recipes by doing a quick search online)
>
> Plastic or other utensils

INSTRUCTIONS

1. Begin by constructing a figurine out of clay that represents the past year's experiences you want to release in the new year. In this case, the new year will represent the day you do this activity. You may decide to construct a single figurine or create a scene out of clay that represents what you hope to leave in the past.

2. With your utensils, carve any words or phrases in the clay that express your feelings or experience during those times.

3. Once both of you have completed a figure or figures that represent what you want to leave in the past, share them with each other and describe what you have created.

4. During the sharing, be mindful not to dredge up any old arguments. When you are sharing, be careful not to place blame or be critical. When your partner shares, this is specifically a time to listen and help your partner process and leave space for their old experiences, not to jump back into a fight, rehash an argument, or defend your position.

5. Once both of you have discussed what you created, destroy it. Get creative and use the destruction as a way to release your feelings. Smash the clay, drop it from a high point, or do whatever would feel best and most freeing to you.

6. Note down the date and time you did this activity as beginning your "new year."

LET'S TALK ABOUT IT

What did you notice about the negative parts of your relationship or your thoughts about your relationship that you've been holding on to? How did it feel to destroy those old feelings and experiences together? Couples therapist Esther Perel, LMFT, has said: "most people are going to have two or three marriages or committed relationships in their adult life. Some of us will have them with the same person."

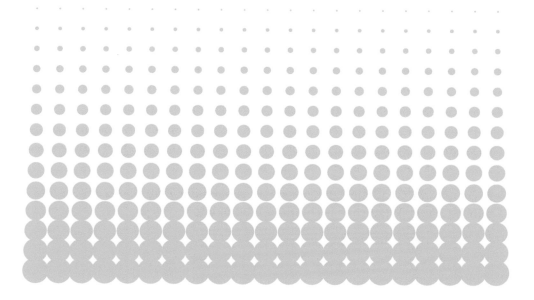

CONFESS TO MOVE ON

Estimated time: **20 MINUTES**

One of the reasons why many couples have the same fight repeatedly is because they haven't spent enough time really digging into *why* and *how* something went wrong. When you rush too quickly to solutions, you miss opportunities to give and hear heartfelt apologies, empathize with each other, and repair what has been broken. By slowing down your conversation around what needs to be forgiven, you both have a better chance of rebuilding a bridge toward connection.

SUPPLIES

INSTRUCTIONS

1. Use the acronym in step 2 to have a conversation about forgiveness. Each partner picks one thing they did recently that hurt their partner and that they still feel bad about.

2. One at a time, go through the actions with each other. One partner at a time acts as the **CONFESS**er.

   C—Confess to the wrong without attempting to make excuses for it.

   O—Offer a genuine apology. Remember to express remorse or feelings of guilt, shame, or disappointment.

   N—Note the other person's pain. Summarize the parts of their pain that you understand. (Example: "I saw how upset it made you when you .... I could really feel that you were ....")

   F—Forever valuing. Reconciling is more important than being right or "winning" the argument. Express what repairing would look and feel like for you. Share what you are willing to do to make things better.

   E—Equalizing. Communicate your desire to rebalance the scales in your relationship. Ask: "What can I do to make it up to you?"

S–Explicitly say that you will never do it again or that you will communicate when you are having difficulty never doing it again.

S–Seek forgiveness verbally. Ask: "Will you ever forgive me?"

3. Once you have gone through the actions, switch positions and repeat the conversation in flipped roles.

LET'S TALK ABOUT IT
Did you feel that you were able to get more closure when your partner was communicating using the CONFESS method? What was it like for you to go through the actions, taking accountability for where you went wrong? No one likes to admit to shortcomings; however, admitting when you are wrong is extremely important in a romantic relationship as it signals to your partner that you are not without fault and will sometimes needs support in overcoming your struggles.

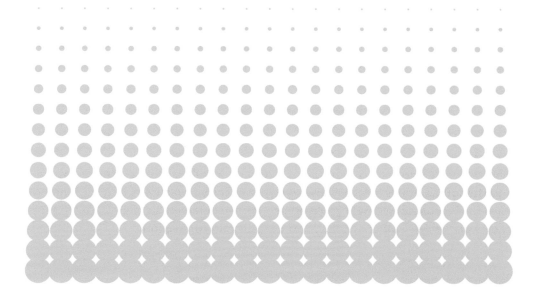

CHAPTER TEN

EMBRACING VULNERABILITY

ONE OF THE most fulfilling parts of building a romantic relationship is when both people work toward gradually showing their complete selves to each other to grow closer together. It's an incredible feeling to feel deeply known and seen by your partner, though this requires both people to embrace vulnerability so they can let their authenticity shine through. There will always be a desire in romantic relationships to be liked by your partner, but this can sometimes get in the way of being your truest self. This can be scary or difficult when neither person can be sure how they'll be received by their partner. When you both take a leap of faith to peel back the layers of your personality, there's always a risk the other person may not like what they find. And yet, without vulnerability, it's very difficult to build true intimacy and strengthen bonds in love. Showing vulnerability is a practice of high risk and high reward. This chapter will help you embrace your vulnerability so that you can get to know each other's authentic selves and deepen your connection.

DOUBLE FEATURE

Estimated time: **ROUGHLY THREE HOURS**

Unless you are one of the rare couples who met each other in childhood, chances are you didn't know each other as kids. Understanding what your partner was like as a child can give you both so much information about how they see the world today, what is important to them, and what they need as an adult. Sharing what you were like as a child is a great way for each person to deepen their understanding of the other, because so much of who you were as a kid relates to who you became as an adult. Getting back in touch with who you were as a child is a wonderful way to start embracing vulnerability, as childhood is often a time when you may have felt completely free to be your truest self.

SUPPLIES
Candy
DVD or streaming service

INSTRUCTIONS

1. Each picks your favorite movie from childhood to watch with each other.

2. Buy your favorite snacks from when you were kids to indulge in while you watch your movies.

3. Spend an afternoon watching both of your two favorite childhood movies as a double feature while you munch on each other's favorite childhood snacks.

LET'S TALK ABOUT IT

What did you learn about each other from watching your favorite movies? How did it feel to tap into your partner's childhood world by eating their favorite snack as you watched their favorite movie? Reconnecting with who you both were as kids can enrich your relationship by giving you a new perspective on each other!

TRUTH OR DARE STARING CONTEST

Estimated time: **20 MINUTES**

Staring into each other's eyes may be the most vulnerable thing you each do all day. Not only does it cut you both off from your usual day-to-day distractions, but there is nothing to do but gaze into each other's eyes and sit with how uncomfortable that may feel. But wait, there's more! This activity is a vulnerability double whammy in that not only does it start with a staring contest, but it also gives way to a game of Truth or Dare, depending on who wins each round of staring. Sometimes, to share parts of your life and your story, one or both of you may need to build a level of trust and transparency. This makes sense, right? It's hard to share yourself with your partner when you're not completely sure what your partner will do with that information. This activity will help you practice building a foundation of trust and transparency so you can eventually take more risks.

SUPPLIES

INSTRUCTIONS

1. Find a comfortable place to sit across from each other.

2. Begin to stare into each other's eyes for as long as you can.

3. Once someone blinks, the winning partner asks the other, "Truth or dare?" Let the opposing partner pick which one.

4. If they pick truth, the partner who won must ask them a question they have to answer truthfully. If they pick dare, the partner who won must come up with a dare for the partner to do.

5. Once the partner who lost finishes revealing their truth or doing their dare, restart the game to play the best out of ten.

LET'S TALK ABOUT IT

How did it feel to gaze at each other for a prolonged period? How did the staring contest influence your participation in Truth or Dare? It's not uncommon to need a level of safety in your relationship before you can embrace your vulnerability. Looking into your partner's eyes is a good way to build that foundation to feel comfortable about sharing more intimate parts of yourself.

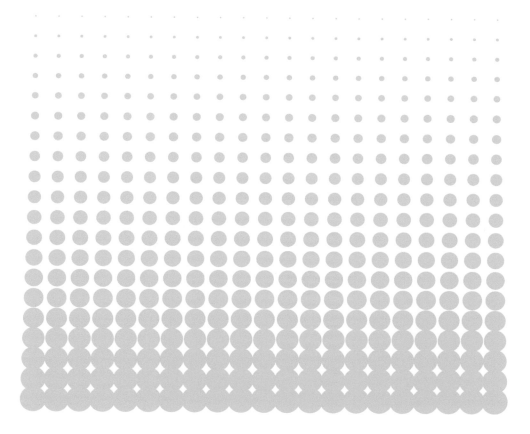

TREAT YOURSELF

Estimated time: **2 HOURS**

Pampering each other is a great way to practice vulnerability of your body instead of your mind. When you allow yourself to be cared for by your partner, you take the risk to let go, relinquish control, and allow your partner to take over caring for you. This can bring anxiety for some who are used to being independent, being responsible for themselves, or being responsible for others. Even though you may crave letting someone else take over, the idea of *actually* letting your partner take care of you may seem great in theory but can be much more difficult in practice. When you switch on and off letting one partner take care of the other partner, you're not only engaging in self-care, but you're also practicing vulnerability by trusting each other with your mental and physical well-being.

> ### SUPPLIES
>
> Foot and/or body lotion
>
> Face masks
>
> Bathtub or foot bath
>
> Bath salts/oil
>
> Massage oil
>
> Tea
>
> Any other spa supplies desired

INSTRUCTIONS

1. Block out an afternoon with your partner and write up a spa itinerary for yourselves. (You'll find examples on page 89.)

2. Each partner chooses three to four treatments they would most enjoy.

3. Consult with your partner on the length of each treatment. (Examples: a ten-minute full-body massage, foot bath, face masks, hair wash/scalp massage, manicure/pedicure, drawing your partner a bath with candles and salts)

4. Gather any supplies that you don't already have.

5. Make your space spa-like by lighting candles and dimming lights, burning incense, and wearing your favorite robes.

6. Take turns being the giver and receiver of your chosen spa treatments. (Example: foot rub for the first person, back rub for the second person, ten-minute full-body massage for the first person, ten-minute full-body massage for the second person)

7. End your spa day with drinking your favorite herbal tea together.

ITINERARY EXAMPLES

Partner 1:

Foot massage

Pedicure

Bath/face mask

Partner 2:

Back massage

Hand scrub

Manicure/face mask

LET'S TALK ABOUT IT
How did it feel to let yourself completely relax into your partner's care? Was it easier for you to be the giver or receiver of the spa treatments? Notice how you felt before the spa day versus after. We tend to think about vulnerability as only sharing stories; however, it's important to remember that your bodies are involved just as much as your minds are in your ability to be vulnerable.

BLINDFOLDED OBSTACLE COURSE

Estimated time: **30 MINUTES**

Depending on the stage of your relationship, putting your full trust in each other may be a daunting concept. When the road before you is unclear—in a relationship or in life—it can be very scary to accept your vulnerable state by trusting the process and relinquishing control. Taking away one of your senses will mimic the feeling of not knowing where you're going so that you can practice trusting your partner's instincts, guidance, and belief that they have your best interests in mind.

SUPPLIES

Various household items

Masking tape

Coin

Blindfold

INSTRUCTIONS

1. Decide on a location for your two obstacle courses, indoors or outdoors.

2. Gather your obstacles. They can be a combination of household items such as chairs, buckets, or any other items you wish to use.

3. Create your courses separately and mark the start and finish line with masking tape.

4. Decide on your rules for how your partner needs to travel from start to finish. (Example: If they mess up, do they have to go to the beginning and start again? What do you want them to do at each obstacle?)

5. Spread out the obstacles you have planned in your course. Keep the course away from anything potentially dangerous like sharp edges, walls, etc.

6. When you're finished building your course, flip a coin to decide who will be blindfolded first.

7. Blindfold your partner and have them go through the obstacle course you made for them by communicating clear instructions to them.

8. Give them a special reward at the end.

9. Switch positions and blindfold the partner who hasn't gone through the obstacle course yet.

LET'S TALK ABOUT IT
What was it like to direct your partner from afar? How did it feel to be the one blindfolded having to rely solely on your partner's instructions? Relying completely on your partner's guidance can feel very vulnerable, but it can also give you an opportunity to practice good communication by building trust that you both have each other's best intentions in mind!

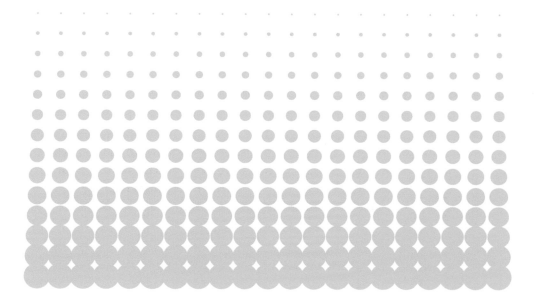

COOKING CHALLENGE

Estimated time: **1 HOUR**

Working together to create a final product requires trust on both sides. It can be scary to lean on each other and accept influence from your partner's perspective, especially if you're used to flying solo or doing things your own way. Consulting each other to complete a task that's outside your comfort zone requires vulnerability. This activity will require you to work together, using each other's strengths to create a meal.

SUPPLIES

Groceries

Timer

Cooking equipment

Plates and/or bowls

Cutlery

INSTRUCTIONS

1. Visit a local grocery store together.

2. Each set your individual timer for ten minutes.

3. Split up and separately choose five ingredients from the grocery store to use for that night's dinner. While you each choose ingredients, don't share with each other what items you're picking.

4. Head back to the kitchen and present your ingredients to each other.

5. Decide on a dish you can make that will incorporate all ten ingredients. You can also use butter/oil, salt, pepper.

6. Cook the meal together.

7. Dine on your meal together.

LET'S TALK ABOUT IT

What was it like to see what your partner had picked? What came up for both of you as you decided on what to cook? The more you can accept influence or help from each other, the more you build an environment of trust and care.

CHAPTER ELEVEN

SHOWING APPRECIATION FOR THE SMALL THINGS

PEOPLE OFTEN GET caught in the trap of thinking that once they reach the next big milestone in their relationship, that will bring them the happiness they've been craving. What often ends up happening is that once you both get the thing you've been striving toward, you may notice that what you want changes into something else completely. For example, desiring an engagement ring becomes wanting to set a wedding date, or wanting to have a child becomes wanting them to get into the best pre-K. In romantic relationships, it's very easy to focus on what you don't have instead of what you do, which can rob you of experiencing joy in the present moment. Celebrating the present moment comes from recognizing and appreciating the small things in your relationship: a bright and sunny morning shared snuggling, bringing each other coffee in bed, a look you share from across the room that only you two know the meaning of. Although it's tempting at times to focus only on the things you want or don't have in your relationship, when you focus only on the bad, you miss out on all the good. This chapter's activities will help you appreciate the small things by increasing presence and practicing gratitude.

GRATITUDE HIKE

Estimated time: **1 HOUR**

SUPPLIES

Hiking boots or sneakers

Active clothing

Spending time with each other in nature is a wonderful way to practice both mindful awareness of your surroundings and gratitude. Mindfulness is about being fully aware in the present moment, which will create an opportunity for you to practice gratitude (also known as counting your blessings).

INSTRUCTIONS

1. Go on a hike for a mile or two. Alternatively, consider sitting in your backyard or a park to visualize exploring a deep-in-the-forest trail together.

2. After you've been walking or sitting outside for ten minutes, each of you shares what you noticed using your five senses: one thing you smell, one thing you taste, one thing you hear, one thing you see, and one thing you touch.

3. After you've noticed your five senses, share one thing you are grateful for in your relationship.

4. After you both have shared, keep hiking or observing nature until you reach the twenty-minute mark.

5. Repeat step 3, but this time add one more thing you are grateful for in your relationship.

6. Repeat this practice at each trail marker until you finish the hike (or every ten minutes or so if you're sitting outside).

LET'S TALK ABOUT IT
What was it like to tap into your senses? Did that impact your ability to think of something you were grateful for? Were there any themes you could pull out from what you both were grateful for? Tapping into the present moment is a great way to begin practicing gratitude for what you love in your relationship.

MY PARTNER, MY MUSE

Estimated time: **1 HOUR**

We often hear that beauty is in the eye of the beholder. People tend to be their own harshest critics, focusing on what they do wrong or poorly versus what they excel or are good at. Chances are that your partner can see many wonderful things about you or your relationship that you yourself may have missed or struggle to focus on. Jumping into each other's perspective can help you learn more about how your partner sees the world. Tapping into your partner's perspective can also show you the specific things they appreciate about you and what you've built together in your relationship.

INSTRUCTIONS

1. Go to an art museum and choose an exhibit.

2. Wander around the exhibit together.

3. Each take pictures (where permitted) with your smartphone of all the artwork that reminds you of your partner or your relationship.

4. After you've finished touring the exhibit, find a comfortable place to sit and show your partner the pictures you took, explaining why each piece of art reminded you of them or your relationship.

LET'S TALK ABOUT IT

What stood out to you about the pictures your partner took? Did you notice anything interesting about the pictures you took? When you leave your perspective to tap into your partner's you get to notice what someone else finds beautiful about you and your relationship, which can balance your own way of seeing things.

EACH ONE, TEACH ONE

Estimated time: **30 MINUTES**

Two people often come to a relationship with very different sets of skills. In fact, one of the times when you may be most attracted to each other is when you see your partner acting in "their element," using the skills that they are most adept at. These times may occur when observing each other at work, speaking confidently about a topic, or teaching a skill they're an expert in. Many of us love to watch our partners behaving confidently and competently, which can remind us of the aspects that first drew us to our loved ones. When you can see your partner in a setting that they're most comfortable in, you have an opportunity to recognize the qualities that you most appreciate. This activity will help you learn from your partner by witnessing their abilities. It will also foster a renewed appreciation for the person with whom you've chosen to build a romantic relationship.

> **SUPPLIES**
>
> Any supplies needed for your skills

INSTRUCTIONS

1. Each choose a skill that takes ten minutes to teach the other person. Make sure the skill you have chosen is one you have taught before, that you may even consider yourself an expert in. (If you are good at magic, perhaps you want to teach a basic magic trick. If you are a software engineer, perhaps you want to teach your partner how to write a simple code. If you are great at cooking, perhaps you'd like to teach your partner how to make an omelet.)

2. Gather any supplies you need to teach your skills.

3. Decide who would like to be the teacher first and who would like to be the student first.

4. One person spends five to ten minutes teaching the second person their skill.

5. Once the second person has grasped the skill with some level of success or understanding, switch the positions of teacher and student.

6. Now the second person teaches the first person their skill.

7. The second person spends five to ten minutes teaching the first person their skill.

8. Complete the activity once the first person has grasped the skill with some level of success or understanding.

LET'S TALK ABOUT IT

What feelings came up for you as you were being taught by your partner? What did you appreciate about them in that moment? When you can witness your partner in an environment that they feel comfortable and confident in, you can experience them with more appreciation for who they are and what qualities they bring to your relationship.

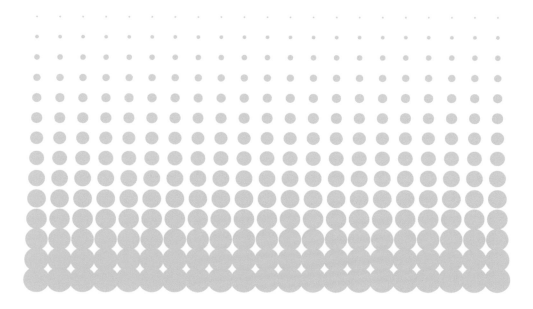

MEDAL OF HONOR CEREMONY

Estimated time: **30 MINUTES**

The longer you have been together, the more likely it is that you've built a shared world only you two understand. Over time, each person has developed different likes, dislikes, needs, and wants. You both also have things that you do for each other that no one other than the two of you may understand the significance of. This activity will help you celebrate the things your partner does for you that only you may acknowledge, understand, or notice. This is an opportunity for you to get creative while showing your appreciation for each other's qualities or behaviors that make a difference in your lives.

SUPPLIES

Ribbons
or string

Scissors

Construction
paper

Markers

Tape

INSTRUCTIONS

1. Begin by cutting out circles in construction paper. These will act as your medals.

2. Brainstorm different awards to give your partner that are specific and unique to your relationship. Feel free to pull from the inside jokes you have with each other or the funny experiences you've shared. (Examples: Award for Best Back Cracker, Snack Queen Award, Stud in Blue Jeans Award, etc.)

3. Write your awards on the circles you cut. Add any decorations you desire to your medals.

4. Cut a string or a ribbon into a long chain that will fit comfortably around your necks.

5. Paste or tape your medals onto the strings or punch a hole and thread them.

6. Agree on a ceremony time when you will present your awards to each other.

LET'S TALK ABOUT IT
How did it feel to think about all the small and big things your partner does for you that require recognition? What thoughts and feelings came up for you as you created your awards? Spending some time thinking about all the things you appreciate about your partner is a wonderful way to build satisfaction and contentment in your relationship.

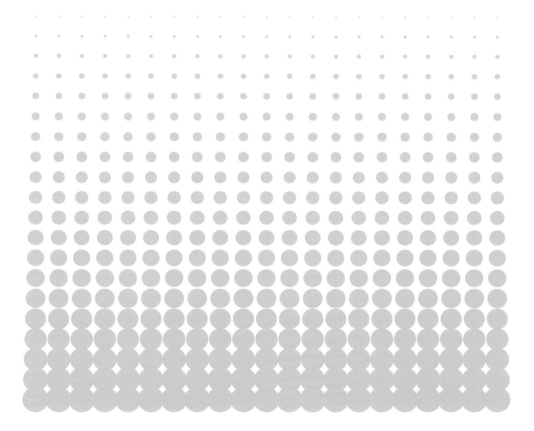

OUR RELATIONSHIP SCRAPBOOK

Estimated time: **1 HOUR**

Reflecting on all the time you've spent together is a wonderful way to look back on all the fun experiences you've shared. No matter how long you have been together, all relationships have small and big milestones that mean something to the two people in the relationship. This activity will help you appreciate the small and large moments throughout your relationship that mean something to you both.

> **SUPPLIES**
>
> Blank notebook or album with blank pages
>
> Collected mementos
>
> Markers
>
> Tape and/or glue

INSTRUCTIONS

1. Gather all the memorabilia together that you'll be putting into your scrapbook.

2. Look for keepsakes from dates, such as ticket stubs, menus, and programs.

3. Print out favorite pictures and text exchanges.

4. Print out a map of the world or a map of your city and mark important places you've been together.

5. Collect any other items you'd like to paste in your scrapbook.

6. Decide how you will display your mementos. Chronologically? Thematically? With certain milestones, such as your first date, moving in together, or marriage? The choice is yours.

7. Spend time together pasting your memories into your scrapbook and decorating the pages.

8. Save your scrapbook as a keepsake for your relationship. Look at it whenever you like.

LET'S TALK ABOUT IT
What memories came up for you both as you created your scrapbook together? What was it like to create a book of memories with your partner? It's easy to get wrapped up in the day-to-day experiences of your relationship without stopping to reflect on and appreciate all you have been through and accomplished together.

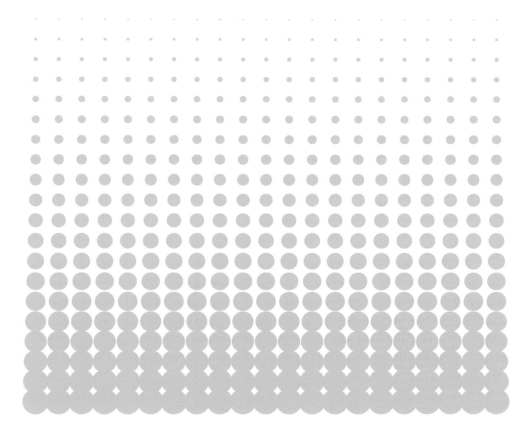

CHAPTER TWELVE

MAKING ROOM FOR "YOU" IN "US"

THE MORE TIME a couple spends together, the greater the chance that their two individual personalities, desires, and experiences will begin to meld into each other. When this occurs, it can be very difficult to know where one person ends and the other begins. Although this level of connection can bring a sense of security, it can also lead couples to overly depend on each other for their own happiness. In any relationship, it's important to maintain a sense of self that's separate from your relationship—not only to remember who you are and what you need, but also to find fulfillment outside your relationship. When couples put too much pressure on their relationship to provide everything for each other, there is an unrealistic expectation that your relationship will solve all your problems and satisfy all needs. The activities in this chapter will help you maintain a sense of your individual selves, allowing you to get necessary space and time apart so that you can come back together again when you both need connection.

SELF-CARE GRAB BAG

Estimated time: **10 MINUTES**

Self-care includes any activity that helps you take care of yourself and is a necessary part of maintaining your mental and physical well-being. Self-care practices are subjective, unique, and personal to each of you: What may be considered self-care for one partner may be completely different for the other partner. Unfortunately, it can be difficult to prioritize self-care when other responsibilities get in the way. This activity will help both of you prioritize self-care so that you can feel like your best selves for each other.

INSTRUCTIONS

1. Tear up your scrap papers into ten smaller pieces of paper.

2. Each write down your top ten favorite self-care activities, one activity on each of your ten pieces of paper. (Some ideas include manicure, nap, massage, yoga, meditation, cooking, seeing a friend, exercise, playing video games, watching your favorite TV show, etc.)

3. Each fold up your papers and put them in your chosen container.

4. For the next ten days, at the beginning of each day, pick out a self-care practice and plan a time on your calendar to do it in the coming days.

LET'S TALK ABOUT IT

What did you learn about your partner from what they listed as a self-care practice? How would you rate how often you both currently prioritize the activities you wrote down? Knowing what your partner does to take care of themselves can help you stay accountable for making sure both of you make time for yourselves.

SELF-ESTEEM POEMS

Estimated time: **20 MINUTES**

Knowing who you are requires you to reflect on what you most like about yourself. When listening to your own thoughts, you may notice that you say unhelpful or even mean things about yourself, to yourself. Negative self-talk can impact not only the way you see yourself but also the way you interact in the world and in your partnership. This activity will help you reflect on the things you love about yourself so that you can remember how deserving you are of the good things in your life. When you feel good about yourself, it is much easier to show up as your best self in your relationship.

> **SUPPLIES**
>
> Old newspapers and/or magazines
>
> Two pairs of scissors
>
> Two pieces of construction paper
>
> Paste or glue

INSTRUCTIONS

1. Each partner looks through the newspapers and cuts out any words that remind them of their best features or traits.

2. Take the words you've cut out and arrange them into a poem entitled "I Am." (Your poem can take any form you like! You can use your name as an acronym and write out your favorite attributes, write a haiku or a free form poem—the choice is yours!)

3. Paste your poem onto your construction paper.

4. When finished, read your self-esteem poems to each other.

LET'S TALK ABOUT IT

What did you notice about the things you like about yourself? What did you learn about what your partner likes about themselves? Knowing what our partner likes about themselves can help us remind them of these attributes when needed as well as help them seek out experiences that make them feel this way.

ABSENCE MAKES THE HEART GROW FONDER

Estimated time: **1 HOUR**

Spending time apart is healthy for your relationship, and it also helps ignite the anticipation and enthusiasm you may have felt earlier in your relationship when you spent more time apart. This activity will help you spend time separately doing things you enjoy so that you can intentionally plan on coming back together at the end of the day with stories to share.

SUPPLIES

INSTRUCTIONS

1. Each decide on a one-hour activity you would like to do by yourself today.

2. Do that activity on your own for the hour. (Some ideas include seeing a friend, playing a sport or video game, getting a massage, etc.)

3. After the hour is over, come back together and discuss how your activity went.

4. When your partner is finished sharing how their activity went, communicate a positive feeling you have about them taking this time for themselves and encourage them to plan a time in the future to do that activity again.

LET'S TALK ABOUT IT

What made the separate experience enjoyable for you? Are you clear on what made your partner's experience enjoyable to them? It's important to take time for yourself. And it's equally important to communicate to your partner that you are comfortable with them going off on their own to have experiences without you.

PIZZA PARTY

Estimated time: **2 OR 3 HOURS TOTAL** (planning, shopping, baking, and eating)

When in a relationship, it's important to consider what needs you have that are your own and what needs you both share as a couple. Confusion and conflict can occur when you're unclear about which needs are specific and individual to one person and which needs you both share. At times, either of you could think that your partner has a need when they don't, or you might assume that a need you have is the same need your partner has. When each person is clear on their own individual needs, you can both come to a discussion understanding where each of you stands. When you start a discussion only considering the relationship's needs or your partner's needs and forget about your own desires, it can be confusing to know what is most important or what either of you is striving for. This activity will help you practice considering your individual needs before you consider the needs that you both share.

SUPPLIES
Paper
Writing utensils
Three individual servings of pizza dough
Pizza toppings

INSTRUCTIONS

1. Plan to have a pizza party as a date night. Alternatively, you could make tacos with various toppings.

2. Plan on making three pizzas—one for each of you and one that you'll share.

3. For the pizzas each of you will be making for yourself, think about what toppings you want that only you like. (This is your opportunity to make a pizza that is especially for you with no input from your partner!)

4. Communicate your desired toppings to your partner and add these ingredients to a grocery list.

5. Discuss what toppings you would like on your shared pizza. Make sure these toppings are ones you both like.

6. When discussing your shared pizza toppings, practice negotiating if you get stuck. (Example: If the first person wants pepperoni but the second person doesn't, the second person might give a counteroffer such as "I don't like pepperoni, but I would be interested in meatball.")

7. Get your ingredient, prepare the pizzas, and eat!

LET'S TALK ABOUT IT

Was it easier to come up with the toppings for your own pizza or the toppings for your shared pizza? In relationships, some folks struggle with understanding what their own needs are and communicating them to their partner while others struggle with being flexible around their own needs for the betterment of the relationship. Which do you struggle with and how does that impact your relationship?

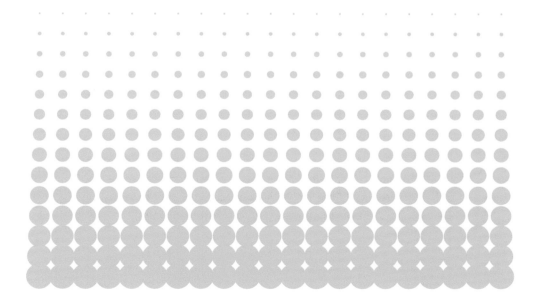

PERSONAL VISION BOARD

Estimated time: **30 MINUTES**

Romantic relationships often provide so much comfort, safety, affection, and satisfaction that it can be easy to forget about your own individual dreams and desires outside your relationship. In this activity, you'll create your own vision board, which is a collection of images that represent your future dreams and desires. When you know what your partner wants out of life, you can act as their biggest cheerleader.

SUPPLIES

Old magazines

Poster board

Glue

INSTRUCTIONS

1. Look through old magazines together.

2. Each cut out pictures, phrases or keywords that represent your individual goals for the next year.

3. Paste the images you found to your own separate poster board.

4. Add any words or phrases that go along with your pictures.

5. When you're both finished creating your vision boards, show each other what you have created.

6. After you both have shared your vision boards, ask your partner what you can do to support them in their vision for next year.

7. Tell your partner three things you need from them to support you in reaching your goals for the next year.

LET'S TALK ABOUT IT
What did you learn about what your partner hopes to accomplish? What would you both need to do to make your dreams a reality? Sharing your goals provides an opportunity for you to support each other in your future dreams.

CHAPTER THIRTEEN

SETTING GOALS FOR THE FUTURE

REGARDLESS OF WHETHER you have just started dating or are in a long-term relationship, setting goals for the future can be a great way to grow as a couple. Many folks shy away from making future plans with their partners for fear of coming on too strong. But in reality, wanting to look forward to the future by making some plans in the present is a very normal human desire. In fact, setting goals in your relationship can strengthen the bond you share, help manage conflicts, and bring a greater overall satisfaction to the life you share. Whether your aim is to set short- or long-term goals, it's important to acknowledge and limit the desire to compare your relationship to others. Your relationship is uniquely yours. What you need and desire in the future is completely up to both of you. There is no right or wrong course to take in a relationship; there is only the course that you decide to take together that leads to you both feeling authentic and fulfilled. This chapter's activities will help you discuss your future goals, make some upcoming plans, create experiences for your future selves, and reflect on what you've already built together.

MASH (FOR ADULTS)

Estimated time: **15 MINUTES**

Brainstorming about your future with each other will help you get on the same page about what you may want for your shared future. This activity is a throwback to an old game from childhood, except now that you're both adults, it's much more possible to make your desired future a reality!

SUPPLIES

Paper

Writing utensils

INSTRUCTIONS

1. The first person writes "MASH" on top of the paper.

2. The other tells the first person the categories to write down that matter most to them for their future. Choose six categories. Categories might include honeymoon location, number of kids, pets, job, salary, car, where you live, etc.

3. The second person gives four options for the first person to write down for each category. (For example, honeymoon location: rent a beach house, Hawaii, hiking/camping, staycation.)

4. The first person adds a terrible or funny option for each category without telling the other what they chose.

5. The second person chooses a number from three to ten.

6. The first person counts out that many options, strikes the option out they landed on, and repeats that process until each category has only one option remaining.

7. The first person reads the results to the other.

8. Switch positions and repeat the steps.

LET'S TALK ABOUT IT

What did you learn about your partner's future hopes and desires? Having conversations about the future often feels scary; however, when you make it into a game, sharing your future goals feels less daunting.

BUCKET-LIST BINGO

Estimated time: **20 MINUTES**

While people often spend a lot of time thinking about what they want to accomplish in life, it's also important for partners to reflect on the experiences and activities that you would both like to accomplish together. A relationship bucket list is a great way to think about your shared values and goals, identify important milestones, and proactively plan some experiences you wish to share over the course of your relationship.

INSTRUCTIONS

1. Start by creating an individual bucket list of all the things you want to accomplish or experiences you want to have in your own life.

2. Share your lists with each other and circle any items that appear on both lists.

3. Brainstorm any other activities and experiences that you want to have together.

4. Finalize a list of twenty-four activities or experiences that you both want to have throughout your relationship.

5. Create a bingo card together by adding these twenty-four activities to a 5 x 5 grid with one free space in the middle.

6. Decide on a reward you can share when you get five in a row and another reward for when you finish the whole board.

7. Keep this bingo card and check off the boxes as you accomplish those activities.

LET'S TALK ABOUT IT
What was difficult about coming up with shared bucket list items? Couples cultivate feelings of stability and security when partners have goals they're actively working toward together.

MISSION STATEMENT WORD FUN

Estimated time: **25 MINUTES**

One or both of you may have been asked to create or work on a mission statement at your job at one point in time. If this is new to you, a mission statement is a paragraph that explains an organization's existence, including its purpose and overall intention. For this activity, you are both going to think through and create your own relationship mission statement. Building your mission statement together will help you put into words what is most important to you as well as what you want your relationship to mean and stand for. When you know what your relationship's values and goals are, it's much easier to act with intention, as you can be guided by your shared purpose.

> **SUPPLIES**
>
> Whiteboard
>
> One
> dry-erase
> marker

INSTRUCTIONS

1. On a whiteboard, use the dry-erase marker to copy the message shown on page 113.

2. Fill in the first blank and then pass the dry-erase marker to your partner, who fills in the second blank.

3. If, at any point, you disagree with what your partner wrote in a blank, stop and talk about it. Decide on a word you both agree on and use it instead.

4. When you complete the fill-in-the-blanks, ask your partner to read the mission statement out loud.

5. Make any edits that are needed.

6. Make copies of the mission statement on paper if you live in separate places.

7. Put your mission statement somewhere that you both can see on a regular basis.

We, _____ and _____ (*your first names*), are devoted to being

_____ (*adjective*), _____ (*adjective*), and _____ (*adjective*)

to each other. We will work to achieve _____ (*noun*) and _____

(*noun*) every day because we believe that _____ (*shared value*). We

are so lucky that we _____ and _____ (*two favorite aspects of*

your relationship). We will remember to keep this front and center even when

we _____ and _____ (*two things you are actively working to*

improve in your relationship). No matter how hard things get, we will never

forget to _____ each other (*verb*). In the future, we strive to create

_____ and _____ (*two dreams you have*).

LET'S TALK ABOUT IT

When are the times you would like to refer to this mission statement? What would make either of you want to add to your mission statement in the future? Creating a mission statement with your partner is a powerful way to verbalize what your relationship stands for so that you can make sure, as time goes on, that both of you are acting in keeping with your overall purpose.

CREATING RITUALS

Estimated time: **25 MINUTES**

SUPPLIES

Calendar app on smartphones or paper calendars

Relationship experts Drs. John Gottman and Julie Gottman believe that couples create shared meaning through their use of rituals. Rituals are defined as patterned, repetitive, and symbolic acts of value. They are the way humans make sense of their world. Rituals can be used to manage anxiety, increase confidence, and instill a sense of order in a consistently changing and chaotic world. Relationship rituals give partnerships purpose and meaning as they help both people along the inevitable ups and downs that come from being in a romantic relationship. Rituals can vary and include anything you do on a daily, weekly, or yearly basis to enjoy your time together. When two people build rituals, they create habits in their connections, which makes you feel bonded to each other.

INSTRUCTIONS

1. Discuss what rituals you already have in your relationship. (Examples may include a weekly date, making breakfast together on a Sunday, quarterly financial check-ins, going on evening walks in the neighborhood, seeing your extended family together once a month, kissing each other when you get home from work, etc.)

2. Discuss what rituals you wish you had.

3. Decide on one weekly ritual that you would like to experiment with or one weekly ritual that you already have that you would like to keep doing.

4. If this ritual isn't already on your calendar, create a weekly recurring calendar invite for this ritual.

5. Decide on one monthly ritual that you would like to try out or that you already have that you would like to keep doing.

6. Put your monthly ritual on your calendars.

7. Decide on one yearly ritual that you would like to experiment with or one monthly ritual that you already have that you would like to keep doing.

8. Plan your yearly ritual.

LET'S TALK ABOUT IT

Did you find that you have more or fewer rituals than you realized? In which areas do you see your rituals lacking? It's natural for couples to prioritize rituals in certain areas, such as caring for children or managing logistics; however, it's good to build in rituals that are for having fun or relaxing together as well.

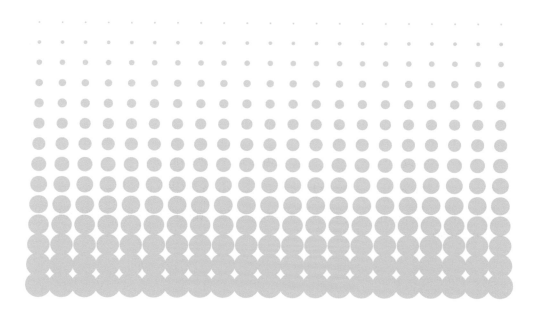

OUR TIME CAPSULE

Estimated time: **30 MINUTES**

A wonderful way to celebrate your relationship is to create your very own time capsule to open at a future date. A time capsule is a great way to capture your current feelings about your relationship, create something meaningful together, and spend time reflecting on all the wonderful experiences you've had thus far. This activity is a way to come together to preserve and celebrate what you have built in your shared life.

> **SUPPLIES**
>
> Relationship mementos
>
> Paper
>
> Writing utensils
>
> Markers
>
> Stickers
>
> Time capsule container
>
> Tape or string

INSTRUCTIONS

1. Find a container with a lid. This will act as your time capsule. The container could be a shoebox, a folder, a mason jar, etc.

2. Collect the mementos to put in your time capsule. Some ideas include favorite pictures, tokens from recent dates, birthday or anniversary cards, pieces of meaningful attire, a favorite bottle of wine, etc.

3. Together, draft a message to put in the capsule. Write down:

   a. What is in the capsule

   b. How you were feeling as you created this capsule

   c. What your favorite parts of your relationship are

   d. What your relationship status is

   e. What you are hoping for in the future for your relationship

4. Decorate the outside of your time capsule using markers and/or stickers.

5. Seal the time capsule with tape or string, depending on the type of container you chose.

6. Agree on a specific date to open it up together. It could be exactly a year from now, or five, or even ten years.

7. Mark this date on your calendars.

8. Find a special place to hide your time capsule away until you're ready to open it.

LET'S TALK ABOUT IT
What feelings came up for both of you as you collected your mementos? What do you think your life will look like together when it comes time to open your time capsule? Looking toward and imagining your future together is a great gift to give your future selves.

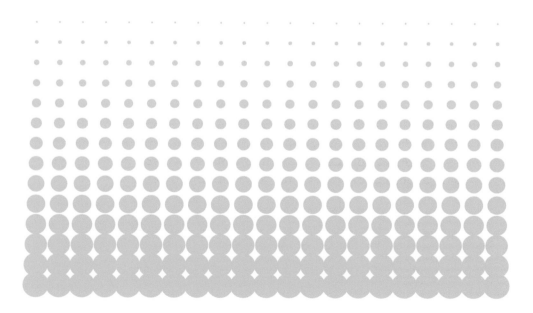

CONTINUING TO CELEBRATE OUR LOVE

Congratulations! You both made it to the end of this activity book! As you moved through this book together, you did an immense amount of work on yourselves and your relationship, while hopefully having fun in the process. Be proud of yourselves. You both have done a wonderful job gaining more understanding of yourselves and each other to build a strong, respectful, and satisfying relationship together. With the activities as your guide, you've reflected on what love means to each of you, you've built a foundation for trust to blossom, and you've learned the ways you both prefer to give and receive love. You've made some intentional plans to maintain your social circles, you've unpacked jealous feelings, and you've discovered new ways of managing and overcoming conflict. You also shared your pet peeves with each other, you reflected on what it means to forgive, and you took steps toward embracing vulnerability to build a deeper bond. You learned the importance of showing appreciation for small things, prioritized your individual needs, and planned some future goals for your relationship.

In all relationships, there will certainly be difficult and trying times ahead. However, you can take all the knowledge you gained here and use it to come back together and give each other what you both need when times get tough. When you put intentional and proactive work into your relationship, it's hard to tell what the seeds of your efforts will grow into. Rest assured that through these activities you both have planted many important and necessary seeds that will allow your relationship to grow into the relationship you desire and deserve.

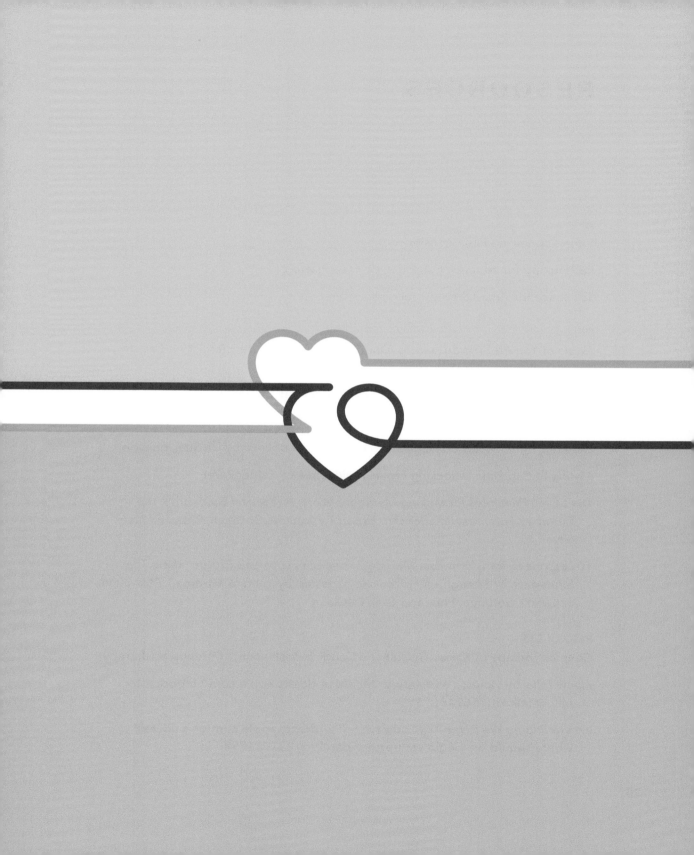

RESOURCES

APPS
Calm app for meditation: calm.com

Lasting app for couples: getlasting.com/counseling

Talkspace for virtual therapy: talkspace.com

BOOKS
Come as You Are: The Surprising New Science That Will Transform Your Sex Life by Emily Nagoski, PhD

The 5 Love Languages: The Secret to Love That Lasts by Gary Chapman

The Happiness Trap: How to Stop Struggling and Start Living by Russ Harris

Hold Me Tight: Seven Conversations for a Lifetime of Love by Dr. Sue Johnson

Mating in Captivity: Unlocking Erotic Intelligence by Esther Perel

The Seven Principles for Making Marriages Work: A Practical Guide from the Country's Foremost Relationship Expert by John M. Gottman, PhD, and Nan Silver

10 Lessons to Transform Your Marriage: America's Love Lab Experts Share Their Strategies for Strengthening Your Relationship by John M. Gottman, PhD, Julie Schwartz Gottman, PhD, and Joan DeClaire

PODCASTS
Couples Therapy by Casey Neistat and Candice Pool: anchor.fm/couples-therapy

Pillow Talks by Vanessa and Xander Marin: podcasts.apple.com/us/podcast/pillow-talks/id1569466131

Where Should We Begin? by Esther Perel: podcasts.apple.com/us/podcast/where-should-we-begin-with-esther-perel/id1237931798

SOCIAL MEDIA

@MelissaFulgieriLLC: instagram.com/melissafulgierillc

@vanessamarintherapy: instagram.com/vanessamarintherapy/?hl=en

WEBSITES

Acceptance and commitment therapy activities and worksheets: positivepsychology.com/act-worksheets

Activities and worksheets for couples: positivepsychology.com/couples-therapy-worksheets-activities

Consent Education: comprehensiveconsent.com/about

Dr. Sue Johnson videos: drsuejohnson.com/videos

Esther Perel blog: estherperel.com/blog/letters-from-esther-31-inviting-vulnerability

Glamour, "Couples Stare at Each Other for 4 Minutes Straight": youtube.com/watch?v=ONYlKmdylXg

Gottman Institute Website: gottman.com

Melissa Fulgieri blog and therapy website: melissafulgieri.com

New York Times, "The 36 Questions that Lead to Love": nytimes.com/2015/01/09/style/no-37-big-wedding-or-small.html

Search for a therapist in your area: Psychologytoday.com and Therapyden.com

SexEd Project: youtube.com/channel/UCcfKnwhTqyydYBkyKop-R7w

Vanessa Marin Online Courses: vmtherapy.com/online-sex-therapy-programs

REFERENCES

Brittle, Zach. "Build Love Maps." Gottman Institute. gottman.com/blog/build-love-maps. Accessed June 3, 2022.

———. "Create Shared Meaning." Gottman Institute. gottman.com/blog/shared-meaning-is-key-to-a-successful-relationship. Accessed June 3, 2022.

———. "Turn Towards Instead of Away." The Gottman Institute. gottman.com/blog/turn-toward-instead-of-away. Accessed June 3, 2022.

Chapman, Gary. *The Five 5 Love Languages: The Secret to Love that Lasts.* Chicago: Northfield Publishing, 1992.

"Cognitive Defusion Activity." Positive Psychology. positivepsychology.com/act-worksheets. Accessed June 3, 2022.

"CONFESSing: Seeking Forgiveness." Positive Psychology. positivepsychology.com/wp-content/uploads/²0²%9/CONFESSing-Seeking-Forgiveness.pdf. Accessed June 3, 2022.

Covey, Stephen M. R. *The Speed of Trust: The One Thing That Changes Everything.* New York: Free Press, 2008.

———. *The 7 Habits of Highly Effective People.* New York: Free Press, 1989.

"Expansion Exercise." youtube.com/watch?v=WRxWr0sFBho. Accessed June 3, 2022.

Gino, Francesca, and Michael I. Norton. "Why Rituals Work." *Scientific American.* scientificamerican.com/article/why-rituals-work. Accessed June 3, 2022.

Gottman, John, and Nan Silver. *The Seven Principles for Making Marriages Work.* Revised Edition. New York: Harmony, 2015.

Gottman, John M., Julie Schwartz Gottman, and Joan DeClaire. *10 Lessons to Transform Your Marriage.* New York: Crown Publishers, 2006.

Green, Celeste. "The Four Steps of Laughing Yoga." *LaughActive*. youtube.com/watch?v=r1v1WvakrYY. Accessed June 3, 2022.

Harris, Russ, and Steven C. Hayes. *The Happiness Trap: How to Stop Struggling and Start Living*. Boston: Trumpeter, 2008.

"Jealousy Toolbox: And Then What? Exercise." Poly Weekly. polyweekly.com/jealousy-toolbox-and-then-what-exercise/. Accessed June 3, 2022.

Lisita, Ellie. "Manage Conflict: The Art of Compromise." Gottman Institute. gottman.com/blog/manage-conflict-the-art-of-compromise. Accessed June 3, 2022.

Loggins, Brittany. "What Is Intimacy in a Relationship?" Very Well Mind. verywellmind.com/what-is-intimacy-in-a-relationship-5199766. Accessed June 3, 2022.

Sheppard, Sarah. "What Is Jealousy?" Very Well Mind. verywellmind.com/what-is-jealousy-5190471. Accessed June 3, 2022.

"A Simple Tool for a More Meaningful Relationship." Psych Central. psychcentral.com/blog/a-simple-tool-for-a-more-meaningful-relationship#1. Accessed June 3, 2022.

Smyth, Sinead. "Accepting Influence: Find Ways to Say 'Yes.'" Gottman Institute. gottman.com/blog/accepting-influence-find-ways-to-say-yes. Accessed June 3, 2022.

Wise, Nan J. "The Rise and Inevitable Fall of New Relationship Energy." Psychology Today. psychologytoday.com/us/blog/why-good-sex-matters/202102/the-rise-and-inevitable-fall-new-relationship-energy. Accessed June 3, 2022.

Worthington, Jr., Everett L. *Forgiveness and Reconciliation: Theory and Application*. Milton Park, Oxfordshire: Routledge, 2006.

INDEX

ACKNOWLEDGMENTS

This book would not have been possible without the support of many wonderful and talented people: Acacia, for finding my writing and connecting me to this opportunity. Andrea and Ellen, for your encouragement and feedback throughout this process. Kevin, for being there every step of the way, in more ways than I can do justice describing here. To my sister, Allie, for editing many of my high school essays. To my Mom and Dad, for believing in education, voracious reading, and courageous writing. To my aunt who taught me that confidence is not a prerequisite to reaching for your dreams. To my beloved girlfriends—Ebie, Christiana, and Ali—for engaging in hours of conversations with me about love, intimacy, and heartbreak, from adolescence to adulthood. To my network of incredible therapists whom I constantly learn from. To my clients, who allow me to bear witness to their deepest vulnerabilities. To every person who allowed me to think out loud with them during this process—I am immensely grateful.

ABOUT THE AUTHOR

 Melissa Fulgieri, LCSW, is a social worker, professor, and entrepreneur in New York City. She owns a private practice providing individual, couples, and family therapy to millennials working to overcome depression, anxiety, and trauma in order to build authenticity and prioritize self-compassion and emotional well-being. She teaches at Fordham University's Graduate School of Social Service. She lives in Brooklyn with her husband, dog, and many plants. Follow her on Instagram at @melissafulgierillc and visit MelissaFulgieri.com to schedule a session, collaborate, or read more of her writing.